Teaching Large Multilevel Classes

CAMBRIDGE HANDBOOKS FOR LANGUAGE TEACHERS

This is a series of practical guides for teachers of English and other languages. Illustrative examples are usually drawn from the field of English as a foreign or second language, but the ideas and techniques described can equally well be used in the teaching of any language.

Recent titles in this series:

Using Newspapers in the Classroom *by Paul Sanderson*

Teaching Adult Second Language Learners *by Heather McKay and Abigail Tom*

Using Folktales *by Eric Taylor*

Teaching English Spelling – A practical guide *by Ruth Shemesh and Sheila Waller*

Personalizing Language Learning – Personalized language learning activities *by Griff Griffiths and Kathryn Keohane*

Teach Business English – A comprehensive introduction to business English *by Sylvie Donna*

Learner Autonomy – A guide to activities which encourage learner responsibility *by Ágota Scharle and Anita Szabó*

The Internet and the Language Classroom – Practical classroom activities *by Gavin Dudeney*

Planning Lessons and Courses – Designing sequences of work for the language classroom *by Tessa Woodward*

Using the Board in the Language Classroom *by Jeannine Dobbs*

Learner English (second edition) *by Michael Swan and Bernard Smith*

Teaching Large Multilevel Classes

Natalie Hess

CAMBRIDGE
UNIVERSITY PRESS

PUBLISHED BY THE PRESS SYNDICATE OF THE UNIVERSITY OF CAMBRIDGE
The Pitt Building, Trumpington Street, Cambridge, United Kingdom

CAMBRIDGE UNIVERSITY PRESS
The Edinburgh Building, Cambridge CB2 2RU, UK
40 West 20th Street, New York, NY 10011–4211, USA
477 Williamstown Road, Port Melbourne, VIC 3207, Australia
Ruiz de Alarcón 13, 28014 Madrid, Spain
Dock House, The Waterfront, Cape Town 8001, South Africa

http://www.cambridge.org

First published 2001
Reprinted 2002

Printed in the United Kingdom at the University Press, Cambridge

Typeface: MT Sabon 10½/12   System: QuarkXPress   [SE]

A catalogue record for this book is available from the British Library

Library of Congress Cataloging-in-Publication Data
   Hess, Natalie, 1936–
   Teaching large multilevel classes / Natalie Hess.
      p. cm. – (Cambridge handbooks for language teachers)
   Includes bibliographical references and index.
   ISBN 0-521-66785-2 (pbk.)
      1. English language–Study and teaching–Foreign speakers. 2. Class size. I. Title. II.
   Series.

PE1128.A2 H468 2001
428'.0071–dc21   2001025090

ISBN 0 521 66785 2 paperback

Contents

Thanks and acknowledgements   xi

Introduction   1
How to make best use of this book   1
What is a large multilevel class?   1
Benefits and challenges of the large multilevel class   2
Eleven principles of coping in large multilevel classes   7

1 Getting to know our students   16

Learning their names   16
1.1   Name toss   17
1.2   Picture it   18
1.3   Names as crosswords   19
1.4   The story of my name   20
1.5   Names and adjectives   21
1.6   I am and I love   22
1.7   Desk placards   22
1.8   Use real pictures   23

Learning about our students' lives   24
1.9   The letter   24
1.10 Guess who?   26
1.11 Three things about me   27
1.12 Mutual interviews   28
1.13 The missing person announcement   29
1.14 Managing my time   31
1.15 Formal introductions   32

2 Motivation and activation   34
2.1   Burst the balloon – expressing opinions   35
2.2   The preference line – explaining yourself   38
2.3   The quick-write   39
2.4   Like, dislike, or neutral   40
2.5   What's your number?   41

2.6   Again and again and again   43
2.7   Friendship   44
2.8   More about friendship   45
2.9   People I admire   46
2.10 Special places   47
2.11 Dreams I have   48
2.12 How I feel now   49
2.13 Slip exchange   50
2.14 Flip-flop books   51
2.15 Frame it   53
2.16 Colored round robin   54
2.17 Circle talk   55
2.18 Teaming up   57
2.19 Needle in a haystack   57
2.20 Optimistic snapshots   58
2.21 Words on cards   58
2.22 A solution for the problem   59
2.23 Student-centered dictation   59
2.24 The seminar   60

3 **Reviewing while maintaining interest and momentum 62**
3.1   Answers into questions   63
3.2   Review posters   64
3.3   Student-made quickie quizzes   65
3.4   Group reviews   66
3.5   Group summaries   67
3.6   Vocabulary wall   68
3.7   Class goals   68
3.8   The KWL procedure   69
3.9   The Venn diagram   71
3.10 Judging people   72
3.11 Running dictation   73
3.12 My sentence   74
3.13 Where is my other half?   75
3.14 Person, place or thing   75

4 **Dealing with written work   77**
4.1   Keep it going   80
4.2   Peer reviews   81
4.3   Writing conferences   83
4.4   Write before you talk   85
4.5   Buddy journals   86
4.6   Using email   87

4.7	Wall newspaper	88
4.8	Using chat rooms	89
4.9	Using web-sites	90
4.10	Writing about landscape pictures	91
4.11	Writing about pictures of people 1	92
4.12	Writing about pictures of people 2	93
4.13	Service writing	94
4.14	A bio-poem class book	95
4.15	The cumulative folder	97
4.16	Sentences into story	98
4.17	Personalized guide books	98
4.18	Change the audience	100
4.19	Clustering	102
4.20	The writing cycle	103
4.21	A resource for self-correction	104
4.22	Letters of advice	105
4.23	In the middle of the story	106
4.24	The spelling list	109
4.25	From words to story	110
4.26	Plot construction	111
5	**Working well in groups**	**112**
5.1	Working together	115
5.2	The quiet signal	116
5.3	Give me your sticks	118
5.4	The text jigsaw	119
5.5	The picture jigsaw	121
5.6	Making mine long	122
5.7	Sentences into story	123
5.8	The aquarium	124
5.9	All for one	125
5.10	Group dictations	126
5.11	The community group project	127
5.12	The walk-about	129
5.13	Picture puzzle	130
5.14	Back and forth movie preview/inview	131
5.15	Three in one	131
5.16	The missing word	132
5.17	Alphabet shopping	133
5.18	Pronoun search	133
5.19	Words to make a cake	134
5.20	Things we share	135

Contents

5.21 Our group cheer 135
5.22 Dictated stories 136
5.23 Three good questions 136

6 **Individualizing and personalizing student work** 137

Individualizing **138**
6.1 Multilevel dictation 138
6.2 The book cart 139
6.3 Silent task work with a self-access box 140
6.4 Working with words 142
6.5 Sentence completion 143
6.6 Question the reading 143

Personalizing **144**
6.7 Vocabulary cards 144
6.8 Three minute talks 145
6.9 The story of my life posters 146
6.10 My object 148
6.11 The vocabulary house 149
6.12 The mailbox 150
6.13 My machine 151
6.14 An important decision 152
6.15 An important sentence 152
6.16 Color sadness blue 153
6.17 Water words 153
6.18 I don't like people who 154
6.19 Careers in my family 155
6.20 What we want from our work 155
6.21 Our own good folder 156
6.22 Words on my desk 157
6.23 Drawing interpretation 157

7 **Making students responsible for their own learning** 159
7.1 What kind of a learner am I? 160
7.2 Setting goals for myself 161
7.3 How a teacher helped me 162
7.4 How can the teacher help me? 163
7.5 How I can help myself 164
7.6 Personal conferences 165
7.7 What kind of a listener am I? 166
7.8 This course will be a success for me if ... 169
7.9 What kind of a reader am I? 169

7.10 Am I brave enough?   171
7.11 Question posters   172
7.12 How do I catch and correct my own mistakes?   173
7.13 Instant answers   174
7.14 Words from the world   175
7.15 Questions on a stick   175
7.16 Many ways to be smart   176
7.17 Grade contracts   178
7.18 Self-check forms   180

8 **Establishing routines and procedures**   **182**
   8.1   Introducing the class syllabus   183
   8.2   Setting up the class calendar   185
   8.3   Checking homework, tardiness, and attendance   186
   8.4   The daily plan   187
   8.5   The absent student notebook   188
   8.6   Exit notes   188

   Class rituals   **189**
   8.7   Lesson starters   189
   8.8   Today's special student   190
   8.9   Celebrating birthdays   191
   8.10 The complaint/suggestion/compliment box   192
   8.11 Elves and giants: an occasional on-going ritual   193

Bibliography   194
Index   196

Dedication

I dedicate this book to my absolutely miraculous first grandson, Adam Jacob Dunlop, who definitely is in a class by himself.

Thanks and acknowledgements

I would like to thank hardworking teachers all over the world. You are my partners in this endeavor. Together we have created that magical space, the classroom – that seemingly mundane territory, where ideas are currency and where imagination and creativity flourish as we continue to serve our students with very practical language concerns.

My special thanks go to my wonderful and ever watchful editor, Penny Ur, who has offered endless and invaluable suggestions, slowed me down, encouraged me, and kept me on track.

I would also like to thank Frances Amrani and Annie Cornford for their careful reading and excellent suggestions.

I am also most grateful to my colleagues at Northern Arizona University both in Yuma and in Flagstaff, as well as my colleagues from Arizona Western College. You have been splendid professional partners. May we have many more creative years together! Finally, a special word of appreciation to Dr. Catherine Medina of Northern Arizona University, who was my listening partner as I was finishing this book and who was able to say just the right words when they were needed.

The author would also like to thank Kate Charlesworth for the illustrations which appear throughout the book and Sue Lightfoot for the Index.

Introduction

How to make best use of this book

- Check the table of contents, the index, and the headings for activities you think are likely to be most useful to you, scan these, and make a note on where, when, and how you will use these activities.
- Keep the book handy in a place where you normally do your lesson planning. Since most of the activities are easy to set up, you will want to refer to this book especially when your time is limited and you need a quick idea to incorporate into the next lesson.
- Although you will probably do the activities as described at first, you will eventually start embroidering on them and change them to fit into your own menu of teaching strategies. That is a sign that they have really become your own. The aim of this book is actually just that – the expansion of your own teaching repertoire.

What is a large multilevel class?

There are, of course, many very different notions of what constitutes such a class. In the language institute where I taught for many years, twenty was considered a large class. Students there were carefully graded into seven levels of proficiency, yet teachers often complained about the great difference between the students who talk fluently but inaccurately, and those who read and write well yet cannot manage to produce a single coherent spoken sentence. Chinese colleagues have told me that they taught groups of sixty or more students in classes where students not only differed in language acquisition ability, but also in age, motivation, intelligence, self-discipline, literacy skills, attitude, and interest, and that such a situation was not at all unusual for them. A colleague from Pakistan tells me that she teaches classes of over one hundred, her only audio-visual aid being a piece of chalk which frequently refuses to write on her small and cracked blackboard. The rooms where she teaches are unheated, and a steady drip from the ceiling during the rainy season can certainly divert the already uncertain attention span of her students. H. Douglas Brown in his *Teaching by Principle* (Prentice Hall Regents, 1994) writes about the possibilities of classes that have

600 students, but notes that while such a number is unusual, classes of sixty to seventy-five students are not so exceptional around the globe.

As we can see, it is not easy to provide an exact definition of what constitutes a large multilevel class. Since all learners are different in language aptitude, in language proficiency, and in general attitude toward language, as well as in learning styles, we can probably say that most language classes are multileveled. Language classes also tend to be highly heterogeneous. That is, students in many of our classes are of different genders, maturity, occupations, ethnicities, cultural and economic backgrounds, as well as personalities. Multilevelness then, as much as class size, is a matter of perception.

In this book, however, I will define large classes as classes of thirty or more students in elementary, secondary, adult, and tertiary settings. I will define multilevel classes as the kinds of classes that have been roughly arranged according to ability, or simply classes that have been arranged by age-group with no thought to language ability. These are classes in which students vary considerably in their language and literacy skills and are in need of a great deal of personal attention and encouragement to make progress. Teaching in such classes may, indeed, be very much like teaching in all other situations, but if so, then teaching in these classes is *more so*! More arduous, more exhausting, and infinitely more demanding. It is also, as I will later point out, infinitely more challenging and more interesting.

Benefits and challenges of the large multilevel class

The benefits

Although teaching in the large class is far from easy, there are certain advantages that we should be aware of.

There are always enough students for interaction

When we teach large classes, we often daydream about how wonderful it would be to teach a small group. However, I have had the experience of teaching very small classes. One particular group consisted of eight young men from the same school in Turkey. They knew everything about one another and were soon quite tired of one another's company. The class settled into a dull pace until one evening, because of the absence of another teacher, fifteen lower-level students from another class joined us. I was amazed to see how the influx of these new students, whose presence made the class infinitely more multileveled, increased the interest, energy-level, and linguistic output of the entire group. Very small classes, I discovered, afforded neither the individual attention of a private lesson nor the advantages of interactive class work. Such problems need not ever be our concern in the large multi-level class.

We get a rich variety of human resources

In a large multilevel class, there are a great many opinions, a great many points of reference, perhaps many cultural backgrounds, many temperaments, many world-views and values, many different experiences and many styles of learning. In ESL settings, students may come from different systems of writing and with a variety of literacy skills. This wealth of dissimilarity can be used to our advantage in creating interesting, varied, meaningful, and student-centered lessons. Students can learn as much by finding out about one another as they can from reading a text, and the immediate interest that such personal contact engenders creates a positive classroom climate that promotes genuine language learning. Chapters one, two, and three of this book give suggestions on how to take advantage of such variety. See, for example, activities 1.15, 2.1, 2.5, 2.17, and 3.10.

The teacher is not the only pedagogue

In large classes, the instructor has a built-in advantage. Since there are so many levels of language ability, it is only natural that the more able students quickly assume the role of teacher-assistants. In such classes, students can learn as much from one another as they learn from the teacher. Early on, we should establish the kind of climate that encourages students to help one another or ask for help from fellow students. Cooperation works better than competition in the large class: cross-ability grouping allows the more able learners to improve their language skills by honing their ability to explain, to state clearly, and to give effective examples, while it provides the less able with considerable support. Such cooperative, interdependent learning will aid our students in fostering a positive mutual reliance and help them to function better in a highly complex, interdependent society. Chapters five and seven of this book are particularly useful in pointing out how peer teaching can be used to promote a climate of cooperation. See, for example, activities 5.1, 5.4, 5.7, 7.5, and 7.8.

We are never bored

Since, as teachers of large multilevel classes, we must constantly be aware of many simultaneous activities and processes as well as a variety of incoming stimuli, working with such classes provides us with a steady challenge. It also summons the best and most effective aspects of both our intellectual and emotional natures. Activities 1.4, 1.5, and 1.10, for example, take advantage of such a variety of processes.

Professional development occurs naturally

Although experience in any classroom helps us to develop our technique, work in the large multilevel class truly forces us to invent and develop new ways of organizing material. These are the classes that compel us to find better ways of setting up routine tasks. These are the classes that make us think, create, and grow as teachers. Chapters two, three, and eight of this book are useful in suggesting options to meet such challenges. See, for example, activities 2.5, 2.6, 3.2, 8.1, and 8.3.

The challenges

The advantages are indeed real, and once we have learned to cope in the large class, we are pleased with the challenges such an environment offers. Nevertheless, the job of teaching the large class also presents us with a great many obstacles.

We often feel out of control

Because the class is so large, we often feel that we have lost authority. Classroom management becomes a formidable obstacle that must be overcome before we can even begin to think about real teaching. The word 'control,' of course, means different things to different teachers, and we can find our own sense of control only when we know ourselves and understand what kind of a classroom ambiance we require. Some of us function best in a fairly chaotic classroom atmosphere, while others feel the need for perfect decorum. I have found that good organization helps to promote good control. Good organization, among other things, helps students to know what is expected of them and to get on task quickly and efficiently. Having a special place on the blackboard where homework assignments are always placed or where directions for the first activity of the day are written, and a place where all the scheduled activities for the lesson are listed, help in establishing good control.

The principles of 'variety' (see page 8) and 'pace' (see page 9) examined below can also help us to establish a sense of security and control. Chapters five, seven, and eight of this book give suggestions on how we can reach the level of competence that we need in order to function with an adequate feeling of composure. See, for example, activities 5.3, 5.14, 7.3, 7.12, 8.3, and 8.4.

In the large class we sometimes feel trapped in the problems of management

Because the classes are so large, a variety of managerial tasks is demanded of us. How do we make a smooth switch from a teacher-fronted to group framework? How do we see to it that everyone knows how to stay on task? How do we make sure that attendance is properly taken without using up valuable class time? How do we ensure that everyone knows what the assigned homework is and that the work is properly checked? How do we integrate students who join the class at a date far into the course? What do we do about late stragglers? In short, how do we make class management smooth and invisible?

A few managerial techniques and workable routines can help us out. I have found that establishing routines for the collection of homework, and the checking of homework, and presentation of certain activities on assigned days, such as dictation every Monday, and/or conversation groups every Thursday, are helpful. I have cut down on latenesses considerably by developing a point system in which everyone who is in his/her place on time with the proper material out for study is awarded three points. In certain classes, I have posted a sign-in sheet by the door of the class. On arrival, students sign their name and the time of arrival. Such self-checking mechanisms promote student responsibility and make our work easier. Chapters four and seven of this book suggest several strategies for smooth classroom management. See, for example, activities 4.3, 4.21, 7.1, 7.2, and 7.12.

We are frustrated by the huge amount of written work

There are two reasons why we want to respond to our students' written work: students need feedback in order to learn, and they want to know and hear what other people think of their written expression. In our large multilevel classes, the amount of paper work, however, is so enormous that we often feel completely overwhelmed and not up to the task. How can we provide the kind of response we want to give our students? The principle of 'collaboration' will once more come to our aid. When properly trained, students can become excellent peer reviewers and editors and learn a great deal about their own writing in the process. Like all writers, students like to see publication of their work. The principle of 'individualization' will help us in creating forums through which students can display and share written work. Chapter four of this book offers suggestions on how to peer review and display written work. See, for example, activities 4.2, 4.3, 4.7, 4.13, 4.15, and 4.21.

It is difficult to provide for individual learning styles

We would like to allow each of our students to find his/her preferred and unique way and pace of learning. The principles of 'collaboration' (having students working together toward common goals, see page 10), 'personalization' (arranging for the kinds of activities that will allow students to express their own opinions and ideas, see page 12), 'individualization' (arranging activities that will allow students to work at their own pace, see page 12), and that of 'enlarging the circle' (including as many students as possible in any activity, see page 14), all point toward allowing students a sense of self in the large class. Chapter six of this book suggests ways in which students can best follow their own learning styles. See, for example, activities 6.1, 6.3, 6.5, and 6.8.

Activating the quiet student is difficult

We often feel discouraged when only a few students participate and we cannot manage activating a great many others, who look and act bored. It is indeed very easy to let those few students who enjoy speaking out in front of the whole group take over and dominate the class. Is it possible to get everyone involved? How can we find ways to keep those who over-participate calmer and more interested in what their fellow students have to contribute? Can we organize group work and pair work in such a way that our students have the best possibility for speaking out, practicing language, getting attention, and experiencing immediate feedback? The principles of 'open-endedness'(see page 13), 'interest' (see page 9) and 'variety' (see page 8), are fundamental to student engagement. Further suggestions on how to activate and involve the class can be found in Chapters two and five of this book. See, for example, activities 2.4, 2.5, 5.1, and 5.4.

Below are some practical principles for coping in the large multi-level class.

Eleven principles of coping in large multilevel classes

Although the problems in large classes can be formidable, they are not insurmountable. There are ways of coping, as well as functional principles and strategies that can turn a struggle into a challenging trial.

Principle one: Scarlett O'Hara

It is well to note that our work in large multilevel classes will never be easy. And there will always be days when we feel frustrated. This is par for the course. Nevertheless, there will always be many more good than bad days. We will always know that our work is important, that through our work we have contributed to the welfare of people and of society, and if today was bad, chances are that tomorrow will be better. If the class we have right now is impossible, next semester's group may be ever so much better. If the material we are working with just doesn't click, we can always choose something more appropriate when we teach the same topic next time.

If you have read *Gone with the Wind* by Margaret Mitchell, you know that its heroine, Scarlett O'Hara, had a special mantra when things got too tense: 'I will think about it tomorrow,' she said. This philosophy may prove helpful in dealing with the frustrations that accompany teaching large multilevel classes. No matter how good we get to be, no matter how much personal fulfillment we may find in our work, there is no escaping the fact that the job will always present us with challenges. In fictional or filmed teacher stories, the hero teacher usually struggles mightily during his/her first year of teaching and then through some miraculous epiphany understands why things have not worked out well. Or, our hero teacher changes his/her tactics/attitude/technique/strategy and presto he/she becomes the most wonderful and beloved teacher in the world. No wonder real teachers get fed up with the stories! In real life, the struggle, in all its various forms, continues throughout one's career. Of course, we all develop and learn many things, but the job is eternally challenging and that perhaps is one reason why so many of us love it!

Because we take our work seriously and are committed to it, the stresses and strains of dealing with a great many people and pressures every day have a way of wearing us down. It is important for us to know that we are not alone in our trials and pitfalls. All teachers of large multilevel classes experience such problems. These are tribulations that go along with the job, but they are difficulties that can be out-lived and overcome. They are to be seen as natural hindrances in an otherwise satisfying career and they are to be dealt with. Occurrences like those listed below are not uncommon in our work:

- Our class is particularly uncooperative, and the harder we try, the more complicated and unproductive our efforts seem to be.
- The class gets out of hand, and nothing seems to calm them.
- The class is lethargic, and no matter what we do, students remain bored and on the edge of total indifference.
- An unpleasant memo from a harried administrator can send chills down our spines.
- A momentary classroom commotion can make us believe that we are useless as teachers.
- A beautiful set of work sheets that consumed much of our vacation time proved to be far too difficult or too easy; we conclude that we have lost all our powers of judgment.
- Judgmental colleagues or thoughtless administrators sometimes offer the kind of advice that displays their superiority and makes us taste our own inadequacies.

These irritants can happen to any classroom practitioner. However, because of the size and volatility of the large class, teachers in such settings are subject to even greater stress and feel more vulnerable. We must learn to shrug off such irritants, or at least do as Scarlett O'Hara did – think about them tomorrow. By the next day, the scalding water may have evaporated into steam.

If we have had a bad lesson – and those happen to all of us – it is well to remember that a bad lesson is just that, one bad lesson. We should not dwell on it. We should not discuss it with our class. It is better to walk into our next class with a smile and teach a very good lesson!

The principles that follow will help us to make our work easier and more manageable and give us ideas in how to avoid and minimize many of the above frustrations and how to teach that next great lesson!

Principle two: variety

Variety is important in all teaching. It is particularly relevant in large multilevel classes because we have so many styles of learning and attention spans to relate to. A variety of activities and techniques is important in all learning situations but particularly relevant in the large multilevel class because varieties of tasks can accommodate different levels in our class. For example, during a vocabulary lesson. Some students can be looking up the dictionary definition of words, while others find sentences in the text where the words appeared, and still others are formulating their own original sentences with the new words.

Students cannot concentrate on an activity for more than a limited length of time. If an activity goes on too long, the mind begins to wander, no matter how fascinating the subject. In large classes such a lack of attention can prove disastrous, so we must constantly vary our techniques and approaches. Variety is extremely important in provoking interest within large groups of students. Those who do not like one phase of an activity or topic may well like the next.

This does not mean that we cannot pursue the same subject matter for an entire hour or longer, but it does mean that we must vary the way in which things are done. For example, if the students have been reading silently for a while, let them join a partner and read to each other. If the class has been very active, it is time for a reflective activity. If the work has been teacher-fronted, we can get into small groups. If we have been working on something very challenging, perhaps it is time to switch to something lighter. The principle of variety will definitely help us to activate the quiet student and to maintain control. Chapter two of this book will explore several techniques for developing variety in the classroom. See, for example, activities 2.2, 2.3, 2.4, and 2.6.

Principle three: pace

Correct pacing means that we should handle each activity and phase of activity at the tempo and momentum suitable to it. Doing an activity too fast or too slowly can ruin the process. This is particularly important in the large multilevel class because without correct pacing, we can lose control and make our students either bored or frustrated, and in a large multilevel class such students become troublemakers and distract even the most fastidious and most motivated. Each class has different demands for pacing, and only careful observation can teach us just what kind of pace to set for our students. As a rule, drills should proceed briskly; discussions that involve thought, reflection, and introspection must move at a more leisurely pace. Through careful practice in large multilevel classes, students can learn how both drill and discussion techniques can be effectively done in small groups. We have to make provisions for students who finish early and create the kinds of activities that allow the slower student extra time. See, for example, activities 2.2, 3.3, 3.6, and 3.8.

Principle four: interest

All of us as students suffered through the endless monotony of boring lessons. In the large class, interest is particularly important because as soon as a group of students loses interest, they are likely to either cause trouble or create the kind of distraction that will focus on them rather than on the lesson. All of us want to be interesting teachers, but just what is it that makes an activity interesting? In my work as a teacher I have discovered three fundamental characteristic aspects of topics that bring about student interest. These are aspects that:

- arouse student curiosity
- tap into meaningful existential questions
- touch students' lives

I have found that it is possible to develop such activities at all levels of ESL/EFL and in a variety of cultural settings. Topics that lend themselves to such activities are:

- management of time
- family relations
- management of money
- friendships
- food and eating habits
- animals
- latest news
- home
- travel

However, an interesting topic alone will not automatically generate appeal for students. To create real student interest requires the creation of game-like activities with clear goals and motivating processes that guide students through involving tasks into thoughtful and insightful use of language. The thoughtful use of attractive visuals, activities that convey and receive meaning, problem-solving processes, personalizations, and role-plays all add to the making of student involvement and student interest. Creating interest will help us both with control and management of our classes. Making our lessons interesting will also insure that as many students as possible stay involved.

The activities in this book have been constructed with interest in mind.

Principle five: collaboration

Collaboration means working together and cooperating. Collaboration is good teaching in all classes: through collaborative learning, students participate more, they learn how to compromise, they negotiate meaning, and they become better risk-takers and more efficient self-monitors and self-evaluators; classroom atmosphere and efficiency improve as does student self-esteem. However, in large multilevel classes collaboration is a must. In the large class, a teacher simply cannot be everywhere at the same time, and cannot service the immediate needs of all students. Students therefore must soon learn to use one another as language resources. Everyone in the room is sometimes a student and sometimes a teacher, and students learn to carry a large slice of responsibility. More able students come to understand that they will learn a great deal them-selves by explaining something to a less able student and by listening patiently while other students make their contributions.

Some of the strategies that help students to collaborate are:

- Group work in which students complete a task together.
- Pair work in which students share ideas or quiz and drill each other.
- Peer review in which students analyze and comment on one another's written work.
- Brainstorming in which students contribute ideas on a single topic.
- Jigsaw activities in which students each contribute different aspects of knowledge to create a whole.
- Collaborative writing in which a group of students collaborate to create a piece of writing like a letter of advice.
- Collaborative community projects in which groups of students in-vestigate an aspect of the community and later report on it.
- Group poster presentations in which groups of students create a poster that demonstrates a topic, an issue or a problem.
- Buddy journals through which students write on possibly assigned topics to a classmate or a student in another class or school and periodically exchange and react to each other's journals.

A word about jigsaw activities:

The jigsaw is most frequently used for collaborative reading, during which a reading passage has been divided into four sections. Individual students are responsible for studying one section, talking about their section with those who have read the same, and then in groups of four, teaching their section to the entire group, thus re-creating the entire reading passage.

I have, however, seen the jigsaw used in many other creative adapta-tions. For example, a teacher of very young children asked individual groups of children to study a fruit and present the fruit to the entire class. Once the fruits were all presented, the class made fruit salad.

In a content-based language class that I recently observed, a mathe-matics teacher allowed his students to study a story problem on four levels of language difficulty and then create a meaningful whole of the problem and its solution.

I have found collaboration to be the best solution for staying on top of the mountains of written work I expect and get from my students because the collaboration causes students to be much more involved in the teaching/learning process and much more helpful through peer- and self-correction.

Chapters five and eight of this book give practical suggestions for collaboration. See, for example, activities 5.3, 5.4, 5.7, and 8.11.

Principle six: individualization

Individualizing student work helps us to deal with the problem of finding the person in the crowd. It also helps to keep everyone challenged, interested, and occupied with tasks that are neither too difficult or too easy.

All students, just like the rest of us, produce infinitely better results when they work on projects that are of genuine interest to them rather than just fulfilling teacher assigned work. In large multilevel classes it is particularly important to provide opportunities for students to work at their own pace, in their own style, and on topics of their own choosing.

There are many ways of promoting individualization:
* portfolio projects
* poster reports
* self-access centers
* individual writing such as book reviews, article reviews, advertisements or diaries
* personalized dictionaries
* student-created web-pages on which students present themselves to the world

A word about self-access centers:

A self-access center, where students can work on aspects of language they need to practice, can be a huge school undertaking with its own personnel. It can also be a simple box of special projects, such as individualized selected readings, specialized vocabulary lists, listening tapes, and pictures that a teacher or a group of teachers have collected and that they take with them to class to have on hand for students who need extra work or specialized attention.

Chapters six and seven of this book offer further possibilities for individualization of students' work. See, for example, activities 6.2, 6.3, 7.1, 7.2, and 7.3.

Principle seven: personalization

It is important that students feel they are related to as individuals and are not simply numbers on a list. It is easy for an atmosphere of impersonality and bureaucracy to overtake large classes. In such a setting, students quickly begin to feel that they don't count and that there is really no point in expressing their opinion, since their point of view is of no interest to anyone. Thus, it is doubly important, in large classes, to provide opportunities in which students may share opinions, relate to their own future plans, explore their ideas on important issues, take stands on controversial topics, and apply their special knowledge to current concerns.

Almost any reading text, listening passage, and speaking activity can be adapted in such a way that it allows personalization. Below are some suggestions:

- After reading about a controversial topic, students can write letters to the editor.
- Students can give mini-presentations about their hopes or dreams for the future.
- Students can investigate the professional requirements of their hoped-for profession.
- Students can create posters of a place they have visited or would like to visit.
- Students can talk about a person they admire.

Chapter two of this book offers such adaptations. See, for example, activities 2.5, 2.7, and 2.10.

Principle eight: choice and open-endedness

You have, no doubt, noticed that many kinds of exercises provided in language textbooks call for very specific answers. There will, for example, be fill-the-slot exercises that ask for one specific word. These kinds of tasks are considered closed-ended exercises. Open-ended exercises, on the other hand, allow students many possibilities for choosing appropriate language items and gearing the exercise to their own level of competence. This is why they work so well in the large multilevel class. Since open-ended exercises are infinitely more success-oriented, they really work well in all classes. However, they are truly a boon in the large multilevel class as they put everyone to work with the new language.

Some ways of providing open-endedness are:
- Giving students beginnings of sentences and allowing them to finish these in an appropriate way.
- Giving students a set of questions and allowing them to answer a specific number of their choice.
- Brainstorming.
- Writing their own definitions of words.
- Matching answers in which several of the matches provide the 'right' answer.
- Questions that can be answered in many different ways.

Open-endedness promotes both interest and correct pacing. Chapter three of this book provides activities that encourage open-endedness. See, for example, activities 3.1, 3.2, 3.3, and 3.9.

Principle nine: setting up routines

In the large class, where so many personalities interact and so much human energy is expended, both teacher and students need the comfort and stability of established routines. The class operates much more smoothly if early in the term certain conventions are established. The following classroom procedures are easily made routine:

- The way attendance is checked and tardiness is handled.
- The way students sign up for special projects.
- The way students are notified of test dates, deadlines and special events.
- The way students check their own reading progress.
- The way students move from a group or pair work strategy to a teacher-fronted framework or vice versa.

While establishing these routines and following them is very helpful, it is also important to keep in mind that no routine is carved in stone. Plans, conventions, and routines are used to guide us, not to bind us. If something doesn't work, it is always possible to examine the procedure, adjust it, change it, or just get rid of it. And while we usually start a new system at the beginning of a year or term, we should not be afraid of starting a new procedure midterm. In the classroom where a climate of trust has been fostered, students appreciate a teacher who experiments with new ideas and who is willing to reject ideas that don't work. Setting up routines helps us to avoid many of the problems of management.

Chapter eight of this book provides useful strategies and routines for classroom use. See, for example, activities 8.1, 8.2, 8.3, and 8.6.

Principle ten: enlarging the circle

In our large multilevel classes, we want to involve as many students as possible, even during the teacher-fronted phases of our lessons. We often worry about the fact that only a few students participate; we simply never know whether those quiet listeners are passive participants or daydreamers who soon may exhibit behavior problems. There are several ways in which we can enlarge the circle of active attention in our classes:

- We should not call on the first student whose hand goes up, but rather, wait until many hands are raised, and as the hands go up encourage greater participation by saying *I see five hands up, aren't there more? Oh, I see five and a half ... oh good, now there are six. I am waiting for more ... .*

- When a student is talking, we have the tendency to walk closer to him/her. It is better if we walk farther away and allow his/her voice to carry across the room to reach more students.
- We should ask a question before calling the name of a student who will answer it, and then not be afraid to pause for some thinking time. Since we ourselves know the answer so well, we may not realize that thinking time is needed before students will volunteer to answer. Silences in the classroom frighten us. They need not!
- We should not call on students in a predictable order, for that certainly will cut down on student involvement.
- It is helpful to let shy students know before the lesson that we plan to call on them during the lesson. It works best if we can arrange a signal that will warn the student that he/she will soon be called on.
- It is good to listen carefully to our students and allow student-initiated topics to 'interrupt our lesson plan'. A student's personal question may well be more interesting to students than what the teacher originally planned. We should remember that we are there to teach language, not necessarily to cover certain material.

When we enlarge the circle, we avoid many of the problems connected to classroom control and interest. Opening up the circle is a principle that can be applied to all the activities in this book.

Principle eleven: question the kind of questioning we use

During parts of our teacher-fronted lessons, we will, no doubt, use questioning – the tried and true method of classroom instruction. In the large multilevel class it is important to ask the kinds of questions that arouse interest and create maximum student involvement.

I have found that the questions that bring about the liveliest responses and keep the entire class awake are the following:

- Questions that begin with *Why.*
- Requests that begin with *Could someone explain to me how ... .*
- Questions to which the teacher doesn't know the answer.
- Requests that ask for clarification and elaboration and start with *Could you please explain that* or *Could you clarify what you mean.*
- Questions initiated by students and moved on to the whole class by the teacher.

You will find some useful question strategies in chapter three of this book. See, for example, activities 3.1, 3.3, 3.4, and 3.8.

1 Getting to know our students

Learning their names

Learning students' names quickly in large classes isn't easy, but it is essential because:

- It promotes good basic human relationships.
- It is helpful in monitoring student records (test results, attendance, assignments).
- Calling people by their names is basic recognition that they are individuals and are being respected as such.
- Calling students by their names helps us to call them to order.
- We begin to feel more comfortable with a class as soon as we know our students' names.
- Students themselves feel better in a class where they know the names of classmates.

Learning students' names is particularly problematic and especially important in the adult education center arrangement, where new students may appear every night. In such a setting, new students feel much more welcome when they are introduced by name and perceive that it is important for them to become familiar with the names of other students. Like most people, students often have strong emotional connections to their names, and we benefit from tapping some of these connections for the purpose of language learning.

A word of warning is needed here. In western cultures people are used to addressing each other by their first names. This, however, is not the rule in many oriental cultures, and an insistence on a first name familiarity can make many students uncomfortable. It is therefore wise to ask for the name students want to be called in class rather than for their first name.

Learning students' names is an activity we need to practice at the beginning of a session. I have discovered, however, that students enjoy doing name exercises throughout the session and profit from continuing to do them.

Below are several activities that can help us to learn students' names.

1.1 Name toss

Aim   fluency practice, learning names

Level   all levels

Time   10–20 minutes

Preparation Bring several soft balls to class (or if you don't have balls, any piece of soft material rolled or tied into a ball shape will do).

Procedure

1 Students stand in circles of 10–15 students.
2 The first student takes the ball and says, *My name is ...*, saying his/her own name as he/she throws it to another.
3 The second student does the same, until all or most of the students have participated.
4 The process is repeated, but this time the student has to say, *Your name is ...* as he/she throws the ball to a student whose name he/she has learned.
5 A volunteer throws the ball around the entire circle, saying, *Your name is ...* as he/she throws the ball to each student.
6 The procedure is repeated with several volunteers.
7 Circulate among the circles to learn as many names as possible.
8 Repeat the procedure several days, always asking students to move into a circle where they do not yet know classmates' names.

Notes

– In classes where desks are nailed down and it is impossible for students to form a circle, students can stand at their desks.
– I have also discovered that classes of adults enjoy this activity. I have practiced it with sophisticated Chinese engineers as well as with Mexican housewives.
– In classes where many new students appear, the name toss can be used often for review.

Variation

I have also used the toss game for learning vocabulary. Each student takes on a word from a previously studied list and the tossing is done just as it was for names.

1.2   Picture it

Aim   learning names, fluency practice, creating supportive environment

Level   intermediate–advanced

Time   15–20 minutes

Procedure

1 Students use large pieces of note paper or stick several pieces of paper together. The paper serves as each student's individual poster. If you have large poster paper available, use it. (See Box 1 for examples.)
2 Students write their name in large letters on their poster and add a picture or mnemonic that will help the class remember his/her name in the target language.
3 In pairs, students explain their posters to each other.
4 Each pair joins another pair, and partners explain each other's posters to the group of four.
5 Circulate and listen to name explanations, learning as many names as possible.
6 Students post their presentation posters around the room, where they stay posted for a period of time.

Optional follow-ups

– Each day 5–6 students explain their poster to the entire class.
– Each day 2–3 students explain the poster of a classmate whose mnemonic they remember well.

Box 1 Examples of explanations

My name is Won Ho. Please remember there is just *One Ho*. There are not two Ho's.

My name is Natalie. I have written it in three syllables *Na ta lie*. That is because I have three daughters. I have drawn the pictures of my three daughters.

My name is Saif. My name means 'sword'. I have drawn a picture of a sword. The last part of my name is 'if'. Remember that *if* I want to, I can cut things with the sword.

1.3   Names as crosswords

Aim   learning names, practicing letter formation
Level   intermediate–advanced
Time   10–15 minutes

Procedure

1 Several students print their names in large clear letters on the board.
2 Other students write in their names as a crossword formation starting with a letter that appears in any name on the board, or they write their names across any of the names using any letter that already appears.
3 As more names appear, more and more letters will be available until all names appear on the board. (See Box 2 for an example.)
4 Students volunteer to read all the names in the name cluster where their own names appear. As they read the names, they identify the students who are called by those names.

Variation

Start with only one name: inevitably sooner or later all the students will be able to add their names, producing one big cluster. The activity thus promotes class solidarity as students will identify with those classmates whose names cross their own.

Box 2   Example of a name cluster

```
R U T H
    A
    M   I
    M A R G A R E T
    Y   I       O
        S       B       S
                E L L I E
                R       R
                T       G
                        E
```

1.4   The story of my name

Aim   learning names, learning about students' lives, talking,
        reading
Level   intermediate–advanced
Time   20–30 minutes

Procedure

1 On the board, write a number of questions relating to the students'
  names. (See Box 3 for examples.)
2 Students stand up and mingle, sharing their name stories with as
  many classmates as possible until you stop the phase. While they
  talk, circulate to hear as many name stories as possible.
3 From their seats, students talk about as many facts as they can
  remember from any classmate's name story.
4 Classmates whose name stories are recalled verify or correct the
  facts.

Box 3 Questions that elicit name stories

Does your name have a meaning?
Why did your parents call you by your name?
Do you know what name you would have been given if you had
been born the opposite sex?
Do you like your name?
Would you prefer another name?
Have you ever wanted to change your name?
Do you get angry when people mispronounce or misspell your
name?
Do you think that your name is part of your identity?

Notes
– In classes where moving around is impossible, students exchange
  information with those sitting next to them, in back of them, and in
  front of them.
– The story about names by Sandra Cisneros in her book *The House
  on Mango Street* (Houston: Artepublico Press, 1985) makes a good
  complementary reading for the name story exercise.

1.5   Names and adjectives

Aim   learning names, vocabulary acquisition (adjectives)
Level   intermediate–advanced
Time   10–20 minutes

Procedure

1 Students think of an adjective that describes them and that begins with the same letter as their name. (See Box 4 for examples.)
2 The first students in each row say their names preceded by the adjective they have chosen. Example: *musical Maria.*
3 The second students repeat the first students' names together with the adjectives and add their own name and adjective combinations. Example: *musical Maria, happy Henry.*
4 The process is repeated until the last students in each row have said all the name-adjective combinations.
5 The last students in each row repeat the name-adjective combinations for the benefit of the whole class. Other students in the row help them if they get stuck.

Optional follow-ups

– Students call out name and adjective combinations of students not in their own rows.
– Students in need of a special challenge are invited to call out the names of an entire row that is not their own.
– Class reviews new adjectives learned.

Box 4 Possible name-adjective combinations

nice Natalie, ambitious Anna, magnificent Mario, particular Pelegrina, busy Bettina, marvelous Mohammed, shy Susannah, talented Theresa

---

Note

Instead of doing the activity in rows, we can do it in small groups. After students become thoroughly familiar with the names of one group, they can form new groups to learn the names of other students.

1.6 I am and I love

Aim learning names, simple sentence practice, vocabulary acquisition

Level intermediate–advanced

Time 10–15 minutes

Procedure

1 Sitting in groups of 10–15, students say their names and the names of something or someone they love. Examples: *I am Ali and I love ice-cream; I am Irma and I love my husband; I am Keiko and I love New York.*
2 Students recall who loves what and call out what they know.
3 Students tell each other whose love comes close to a fondness of their own and explain why.

Variation

You can also use *I am and I am afraid of* or *I am and I hate* in the same manner.

1.7 Desk placards

Aim learning names, taking attendance

Level beginners–advanced

Preparation Before your first class make 5″ by 18″ (12 cm by 46 cm) two-sided placards that are folded in the middle so that they can stand. Make one placard for each student. On one side print each student's name in bold letters. If your office provides student pictures, paste the picture of each student next to his/her name.

Procedure

1 As students enter your class, ask what their name is and have them find their own placard.
2 Students place their placards on their desks in front of them where you can see them.
3 Continue the procedure for as many lessons as you need to learn students' names.

Notes

– You know who is absent by seeing who has not picked up his/her placard.
– My colleague who teaches classes of ninety in Japan told me that his placards are in place the entire semester.

Acknowledgement

I learned this strategy from Dawn Yonally, whom I met at the TESOL 1996 conference in Chicago.

1.8   Use real pictures

Aim	writing, fluency practice, learning names
Level	all levels
Time	fluid
Preparation	Bring camera to class.

Procedure

1 On the first day of class bring a camera loaded with enough film to take a picture of every single student in your class.
2 Have the pictures developed and bring them to class.
3 Students write their names and something to remember them by on the back of their own pictures.
4 Students mingle and tell one another what they have chosen to be remembered by.
5 With the whole class, volunteers share names they recall and what helped to spark their memory.
6 Collect all the pictures and study them.
7 Use the pictures to call attendance until you are sure of all the names.

Learning about our students' lives

Students appreciate a teacher who takes an interest in their likes and dislikes, their special interests and their difficulties. Knowing our students as human beings helps us to see the larger picture of their lives and explains many behaviors that we might otherwise consider unreasonable. Knowing our students is the best preventative medicine for discipline problems.

In large classes giving individual attention is extremely difficult, but it is not impossible and may not take the enormous amount of time we sometimes believe it must. Sometimes individual attention is a matter of attitude rather than a matter of time. Many language acquisition activities offer us the opportunity to know our students better. Below are some activities of this type.

1.9 The letter

Aim	getting acquainted, reading, writing
Level	intermediate–advanced
Time	20–30 minutes
Preparation	Write a letter about yourself to your students. Reveal as much about yourself as you feel comfortable doing. Write about the same things that you would like your students to tell you about. Make enough copies of the letter for the students in your class. (See Box 5 for an example of a letter.)

Procedure

1 Hand out copies of your letter and read it out loud; make sure that it's understood.
2 Ask students to write you a letter about themselves. It can be written on the back of your letter. Explain that these letters will not be graded and may not be returned. The purpose of the letters is to know each other better.
3 Collect the letters and later prepare a 'guess who' activity for the next class (see 1.10 below for 'guess who' procedure), or write a brief answer to each letter.

Notes

– If you don't have enough class time, assign the letter for homework.
– Even in very large classes, reading these letters is not difficult and does not take a great deal of time, because you don't have to mark

them or comment on them and the letters are usually interesting. Some teachers, however, feel the need to answer these letters and this can, of course, be done.

– I keep the letters as long as I have the students in my class and reread them before conferences with parents or students.

Box 5 Example of letter to students

Dear Student,

My name is Natalie Hess, and I have taught ESOL (English to speakers of other languages) for many years and in many countries. I really love my work because through it I get a chance to do two of my favorite things: talking to people and reading books. My work takes up most of my time, but when I don't work I love to cook, to ride my bicycle, to swim, and to read. I feel very close to my family.

I am afraid of mice and I love eating chocolate. I hate tests!

For me, spelling has always been the hardest part of learning a language. That's because I am not a visual learner. I think that a classroom is an exciting place because there is always a great exchange of ideas going on.

I am glad that you are in this class. Please write me a bit about yourself.

Sincerely, Natalie

Sample of student answer

Dear Natalie,

Thank you for your nice letter. My name is Kumiko and I am from Osaka, Japan. Have you ever been to Japan? I have a little sister and a dog. The dog's name is Puppy and she is very cute. My sister and I fight a lot, but now that I am in America I miss her. I am glad to be in your class. I hope to learn a lot!

Sincerely, Kumiko

1.10 Guess who?

This activity serves as a good follow-up to the previous letter-writing procedure.

Aim	getting acquainted, fluency practice, question formation, reading
Level	intermediate–advanced
Time	20–30 minutes
Preparation	Read through the letters your students have written, underlining a particularly interesting aspect of each letter. Make up a Guess Who Chart. (See Box 6 for an example.) Try to choose aspects of your students' lives that you are quite sure they would not mind sharing. If you have any doubt, check with the student before class.

Procedure

1 Hand out the Guess Who Chart to the class that has written the letters, and practice question formation.
2 Students mingle to find out the answers to the 'guess who' questions. To do this right, they should ask questions correctly.
3 When they find a person, they should ask for that person's signature next to the statement that identifies the student.

Optional follow-up

Students get back to their seats and, in plenary, talk about who has done what. During this discussion more details are added to the brief Guess Who Chart information. Example: *Elena has visited London five times. What did you like best about London, Elena?*

Variations

– If you would rather not use the letter as a disclosure, you can simply ask students to write one interesting fact about themselves that they don't mind sharing and use these for the 'guess who' procedure or use the forms they fill in in activity 1.15.
– You can also use the 'guess who' activity to review material. For example, *Find someone who knows the capital of Saudi Arabia. Find someone who knows which is the largest river in Africa.*

Note

The 'guess who' activity helps you to get to know students better and allows them to get to know each other. It never fails in creating a pleasant ambiance.

Box 6 Example of guess who chart

Guess who. . .
1 has been in London five times.
2 has five sisters.
3 has never eaten ice-cream.
4 has been married three times to the same man.
5 learned to speak Japanese fluently at age 52.
6 loves his/her uncle better than his/her father.
7 is afraid of flying.
8 is afraid of mice.
9 plays piano like a professional.
10 plays the drums.
11 hates to study.
12 gets nervous before tests.

1.11 Three things about me

Aim   getting acquainted, fluency practice
Level beginners–advanced
Time 10–15 minutes

Procedure

1 Students write down three interesting facts about themselves.
2 Students get up and mingle. They tell one fact about themselves to three different classmates. (See Box 7 for examples.) Each time a fact matches something in the life of the classmate, that classmate acknowledges by saying, *This happened to me too when ...* or *I have two big brothers too.* Students continue mingling until they have found three classmates who have similar information.
3 The students who finish early can continue mingling and listening to information about classmates until you stop this phase.
4 Students return to their seats and share any information they have learned with the person sitting next to them.
5 Volunteers speak to the whole class about interesting information they have learned about various classmates.

Box 7 Examples of facts one can talk about

I have seven sisters. I went to Disneyland during the vacation. I am on a diet and have lost seven kilos. I love snakes. I have a dog called Panda. I have been married three times. I have five grandchildren. My mother was a beauty queen. I worked as a chicken plucker.

Variation

In classes where moving around is impossible, students exchange information with those sitting next to them, in back of them, and in front of them.

1.12 Mutual interviews

Aim	getting acquainted, fluency practice, listening, speaking
Level	intermediate–advanced
Time	20–30 minutes
Preparation	Prepare an interview suitable to your students or use one of those provided. (See Box 8 for examples.)

Procedure

1 Make sure students know what an interview is (a guided conversation).
2 Talk with your students about when and why interviews are used (radio, television, newspaper, before jobs, etc.).
3 Students sit in pairs facing each other.
4 They take turns interviewing each other. They are not to take notes; they are only to listen carefully.
5 Each pair joins another pair, and each interviewer introduces his/her partner to the foursome.
6 Volunteers introduce their partners to the entire class.

Box 8 Examples of interviews

Initial interview
Tell me about your family.
Can you tell me why it is important for you to learn English?
Please tell me about a future plan.
What do you enjoy doing in your spare time?
Please tell me about your city or your neighborhood.

Later interview
Please tell me about a dream you often have.
Could you tell me about something that you are proud of.
Tell me about a hope that you have for the next five years.
Please tell me about something that you believe in.
What would you do if you had a great deal of money and had to spend it on yourself?
Is there a book or a film that has made an impression on you?
Tell me about a person you admire.

Variations
– You can turn this exercise into a writing activity by having students take notes and later write a story about the person they have interviewed.
– Interviews can be constructed around any interesting reading passage the students might have done.

1.13 The missing person announcement

Aim	getting acquainted, fluency practice, speaking, listening, writing
Level	beginners–advanced
Time	20–30 minutes

Preparation If you have English language newspapers available, look for missing person announcements and bring some to class.

Procedure

1 Talk with your class about when and why missing person announcements are needed, and what goes into the making of a missing person announcement. A missing person description usually includes a physical description – height, weight, color of hair, age if known, color of eyes, identifying marks – typical mannerisms, typical pastimes, dress when last seen.

2 In pairs students create a missing person announcement of each other. (See Box 9 for an example.) They may if they wish draw a picture of their missing person, but they are **not** to write the missing person's name. They may refer to the missing person as X. *Make it very clear that **only positive terminology is allowed** in the descriptions.* Tell your students not to use words and/or expressions that would make anyone feel bad.

3 Students post their missing person announcements on the walls of the class.

4 Students walk about reading the announcements and guessing who the missing persons are.

5 From their seats students call out their guesses and other students either verify or negate them.

6 Posters are taken down and volunteers call out descriptions they remember, while students guess who the descriptions refer to.

Box 9 Example of missing person announcement

Have you seen my good friend X?
She was last seen reading studiously in the library.
She is about six feet tall (183 cm) and looks like a model.
She has long brown hair and a little brown mark on top of her left eyebrow.
Her eyes are green and very lovely.
When I saw her last she was wearing a brown skirt and a plaid shirt and she had her hair tied back in a pony tail.
She likes to laugh a lot and she can often be seen eating ice-cream.
Here is a picture of my friend. I hope you can help me find her. (Students who wished to do so drew a picture.)

Note

For beginners' classes pre-teach vocabulary for body parts and clothing.

Variation

Missing person's charts work very well as aspects of character study when working with a piece of literature or when discussing historical figures.

1.14 Managing my time

    Aim   getting acquainted, time management, fluency practice, speaking, listening

    Level   intermediate–advanced

    Time   30–40 minutes

Procedure

1 Students draw a circle which represents the twenty-four hours of an average day in their lives. They divide the circle into parts and label each part. A third of the circle (eight hours) is automatically labelled *sleep*. (See Box 10 for an example.)
2 Students fill in the other sixteen hours with things they do during the day.
3 In pairs students explain their circle time charts to each other.
4 Students tell each other whether or not they are satisfied with the way they manage their time.
5 Students seek advice on how they can manage their time better.
6 Teacher collects advice from volunteers and writes it on the blackboard.

Box 10 Example of a time chart

1.15 Formal introductions

Aim	getting acquainted, speaking
Level	intermediate–advanced
Time	20–30 minutes
Preparation	Make copies for all your students of the form in Box 11.

Procedure

1 Ask students to fill in the questionnaire on the next page.
2 Collect completed questionnaires.
3 Several volunteers come forward. Each picks a filled-in form from the stack.
4 The volunteers are allowed two minutes to study the information on the questionnaires, while other students are put to work on any kind of review exercise.
5 The volunteers introduce the classmates whose questionnaires they picked to the entire class.
6 The classmates who were introduced acknowledge the introduction with a few brief words. Examples: *Thank you for that nice introduction, Sandra. Thank you, Lisa, you remembered everything about me. Thank you, Jose, it was nice to hear about myself.*
7 Teacher keeps the filled-in questionnaires for future use. For example, they can be kept and used whenever students give a presentation, participate in a debate, present a summary of something they have read, read a composition out loud, or act out a scenario or a role-play before the entire class.

Box 11 Biographical questionnaire

Your name ....

Your country ....

Your city ....

A hope or a plan you have for the future ....

....

Something about your family ....

....

....

Something you are proud of ....

....

A hobby or special interest ....

....

The reason you are studying English ....

....

....

Anything else that you would like to say about yourself

....

....

....

2   Motivation and activation

One of our tasks as language teachers is to get students to express their own ideas and opinions both in speech and in writing. This is particularly important in the large multilevel class, where students often feel lost in the crowd and where there are so many students that a teacher might have the tendency to just listen to those who demand attention. Speaking about one's own ideas and outlook makes one feel much more at home in the large forum. Many students, however, are reluctant to express their opinions, partly because they cannot do so adequately in the new language. I learned this the hard way when one of my reluctant speakers once told me, 'You never hear what I say. You just hear the mistakes I make.'

Students in large multilevel classes are also afraid to speak up because they think they will say something stupid in front of an uncaring crowd, or that what they have to say is not important, or that they really have nothing useful to contribute. Students in large multilevel classes have been heard to say, 'Oh, I don't count. I'm just a number here.'

Our job as language teachers is to help students gain competence in language and to provide the support and encouragement that will raise their confidence and motivation. We must assure students that what they think really matters to us more than the way they express themselves. Once people have something to say, they generally are motivated to find the best way to say it.

If we really want to convince our students that their ideas are worthwhile, we should not only pay lip service to such a notion but also structure activities that promote a genuine exchange of ideas and good thinking. As a rule, students are interested in sharing what is on their minds and are waiting for a chance to do so. If our large multilevel class becomes a community, where students feel safe and where their opinions are valued, they will be willing and able to produce relevant language and to exchange opinions with classmates. If we intersperse many idea-sharing activities with strategies that bring about meaningful language, we can hope that language and communication eventually will coincide.

When I structure activities for activation and opinion exchange, I try to keep the following in mind:

- It is not necessary for the teacher to hear everything that is being said or see everything that is being written.
- Students should be allowed to talk about issues of real interest to them.
- The activity should offer many choices of expression.

The following activities will help to give students the push towards self-expression and interactions with fellow students.

2.1 Burst the balloon – expressing opinions

Aim	speaking, expressing opinions
Level	intermediate–advanced
Time	20–30 minutes
Preparation	Choose an interesting and/or controversial subject. See Boxes 12, 13, and 14 for suggested topics, or create your own. Write each sentence in a balloon or a circle. Place the balloons randomly all over a page and make enough copies of the page for your class.

Procedure

1 Hand out the balloon papers.
2 Read each statement slowly, and ask students to write the words *agree*, *disagree*, or *not sure* next to each statement.
3 Students 'blow one of the balloons up bigger' – that is, they choose and consider the first statement that they want to discuss with a partner. This is a statement that they agree with.
4 Students stand and mingle cocktail-party style. They stop to talk about the balloon they have 'blown up' with the first classmate they encounter, and then move on to another classmate and discuss another balloon.
5 Ask students to find the balloon they disagree with the most and 'burst' that balloon by putting an X through it.
6 Students vote on the balloon that was burst most frequently, and on the balloon that was blown up bigger most frequently.
7 In plenary, students explain why one was the most frequently 'burst' or 'blown up' balloon.
8 Encourage dissenting opinions.

Notes

– In rooms where chairs cannot be moved, students can speak with those who sit next to them, and to the person in front of them. If pair faces pair, there will be groups of four in which students can exchange opinions.
– If you do not have access to duplicating facilities, put balloon statements on the board.

Variation

Students can speak first with someone who agrees with their opinion on a topic, and later try to convince someone who disagrees.

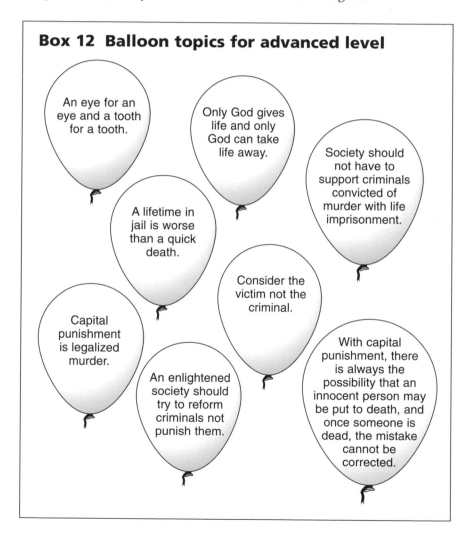

Box 12 Balloon topics for advanced level

An eye for an eye and a tooth for a tooth.

Only God gives life and only God can take life away.

Society should not have to support criminals convicted of murder with life imprisonment.

A lifetime in jail is worse than a quick death.

Consider the victim not the criminal.

Capital punishment is legalized murder.

An enlightened society should try to reform criminals not punish them.

With capital punishment, there is always the possibility that an innocent person may be put to death, and once someone is dead, the mistake cannot be corrected.

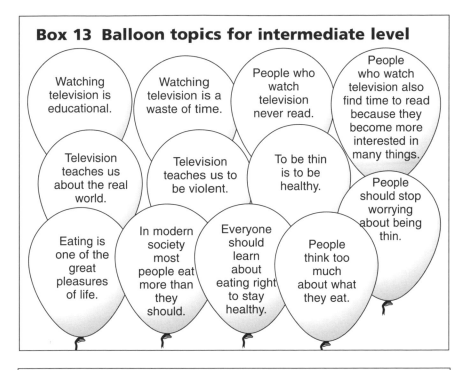

Box 13 Balloon topics for intermediate level

Watching television is educational.

Watching television is a waste of time.

People who watch television never read.

People who watch television also find time to read because they become more interested in many things.

Television teaches us about the real world.

Television teaches us to be violent.

To be thin is to be healthy.

People should stop worrying about being thin.

Eating is one of the great pleasures of life.

In modern society most people eat more than they should.

Everyone should learn about eating right to stay healthy.

People think too much about what they eat.

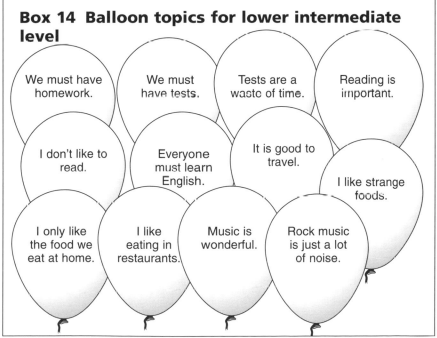

Box 14 Balloon topics for lower intermediate level

We must have homework.

We must have tests.

Tests are a waste of time.

Reading is important.

I don't like to read.

Everyone must learn English.

It is good to travel.

I like strange foods.

I only like the food we eat at home.

I like eating in restaurants.

Music is wonderful.

Rock music is just a lot of noise.

37

2.2 The preference line – explaining yourself

Aim	fluency practice, expressing opinions, a cohesive classroom atmosphere
Level	intermediate–advanced
Time	20–30 minutes

Preparation Choose any topic on which students can express a preference and draw a line on the board to represent the scale of preference. At both ends of the line write two preference possibilities. For example, in a discussion about loyalty, I placed *family* at one end of the line, *society* at the other end. See Box 15 for suggested topics or create your own.

Procedure

1 Students from one row or section of the class come to the board and write their names along the line where they feel that they belong.
2 Students take turns standing in front of their names and explaining why they put their names in a certain position.
3 Volunteers from the class may ask questions.
4 A new row or group of students comes to the board to write their names.
5 The procedure is repeated and can be repeated as long as the class is interested and involved.

Variations

– You can use this line for the placement of characters students meet in literature or historical figures.
– Each row of students can function as a line in which students stand where they think they belong, and explain their position.

Extension

Students write a short composition called *Where I stand*. The compositions are posted on the walls of the class and students circulate writing positive comments or questions on the work of classmates.

Box 15 Suggested topics

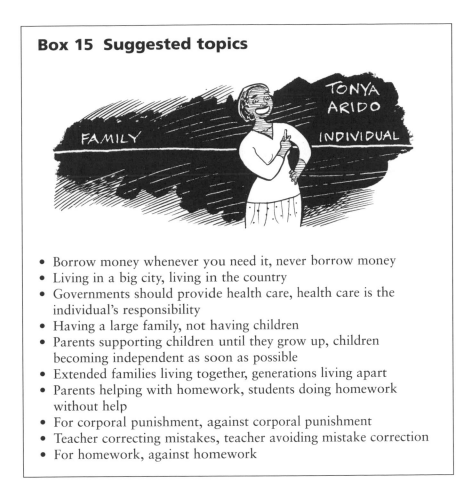

- Borrow money whenever you need it, never borrow money
- Living in a big city, living in the country
- Governments should provide health care, health care is the individual's responsibility
- Having a large family, not having children
- Parents supporting children until they grow up, children becoming independent as soon as possible
- Extended families living together, generations living apart
- Parents helping with homework, students doing homework without help
- For corporal punishment, against corporal punishment
- Teacher correcting mistakes, teacher avoiding mistake correction
- For homework, against homework

2.3 The quick-write

Aim	fluency practice, writing, expressing opinions, a cohesive and cooperative classroom community
Level	intermediate–advanced
Time	20–30 minutes
Preparation	Think of a topic that your class has dealt with, or a topic that needs review, or any topic that you want to introduce. Start a sentence on any aspect of that topic and have this partial sentence ready for dictation. Example: *When I think about my home town, I remember ...*

Procedure

1 Dictate the sentence.
2 Students continue writing.
3 They are not to lift pen from paper. If they can't think of what to say they may continue writing loops or they may write *I don't know what to write … I don't know what to write* until the next idea strikes them.
4 Students write until you stop them.
5 In small groups, students read what they have written to one another.
6 In the groups, students choose the most interesting piece of writing and a student other than the writer reads the chosen piece to the class.

2.4   Like, dislike, or neutral

Aim   fluency practice, expressing opinions, sharing ideas, a cohesive and cooperative classroom community

Level   intermediate–advanced

Time   15–20 minutes

Preparation   Think of any topic that might be of interest to your students and that they might have strong feelings about. (See Box 16 for suggested topics.)

Procedure

1 Assign different areas in your classroom to be the designated places for *I like*, *I dislike*, and *I feel neutral about*.
2 Explain the concept *neutral*.
3 Write your chosen topic on the board.
4 Students move to the area of the class that suits them the most.
5 Students talk to classmates in their chosen area, explaining why they like, dislike or feel neutral about the topic.
6 Students pair up with a classmate from another area and try to convince each other about the rightness of their position.
7 Students return to their own area and tell partners what they heard from people who had another opinion.
8 Students return to their seats and volunteers talk about why they changed or did not change their opinions.

Box 16 Suggested topics

- Big cities
- Woods
- Airports
- Learning new languages
- Night school
- Parties
- Making a speech
- Writing letters
- Using email
- Making friends on the internet
- Eating in restaurants
- Large classes
- Meeting new people
- Eating meat

2.5   What's your number?

Aim	reading, speaking, listening, exchanging opinions, a cohesive and cooperative classroom community
Materials	self-stick notes or tape
Level	all levels
Time	20–30 minutes
Preparation	Write a set of statements about a topic that your class has recently discussed. The statement should express varying opinions on the topic. (See Boxes 17, 18, and 19 for examples.) Number each topic. Make several copies of your list and post these lists on the walls of your classroom.

Procedure

1 Students stand and go to read the lists.
2 They choose two sentences they agree with and write the numbers of these topics on a self-stick note or piece of paper that they pin on a visible place on themselves.
3 Students mingle, finding someone who has chosen at least one topic number which is the same as theirs.

4 Students stand together and talk about their topic. They explain to one another why they agree with the sentences they have chosen.
5 The procedure is repeated with another partner.
6 Students find someone who has completely different numbers. They explain their opinion to each other and try to convince each other.
7 The procedure is repeated.
8 Students return to seats and volunteers explain which sentences they chose and why they might have changed their opinion.

Note

Since students might not remember what their sentence is once they have written down their number, they will return to the posted lists together with their partner, thus creating another reading opportunity.

Box 17 Topics for advanced students

1 Nobody can stop the process of pollution.
2 Schools must teach children how to save the environment.
3 The government should force people to recycle.
4 Every city should encourage people to walk and to ride bicycles.
5 The danger of pollution has been exaggerated.
6 We should try to save all animal species.
7 It is good if some animals which are dangerous and useless, like wolves, disappear.
8 Nobody should be allowed to drive in a car that just has one person in it.
9 There should be special fast lanes on roads for people who drive cars full of passengers.

Box 18 Topics for intermediate students

1 Cars make trouble.
2 We must save some animals.
3 We need clean water.
4 Buses and trains are better than cars.
5 There are too many big cities.
6 There should be a place to throw things away on every street.
7 Cars are the best way to get somewhere.

Box 19 Topics for beginner students

1 Don't throw trash in the street.
2 Take good care of animals.
3 Walk or ride a bike to school.
4 It is good to have clean air and water.
5 Some animals are bad for people.
6 We like a clean school.
7 Life in big cities is good.

2.6 Again and again and again

Aim to share information, speaking, reading, writing, listening

Level intermediate–advanced

Time 20–30 minutes

Procedure

1 Students are assigned different sections of a reading passage or different articles for individual reading.
2 Students make an outline of what they have read. (For a shape of an outline see Box 20.) If this outline form is too formal, students can simply make a list of the important ideas.
3 Students stand and mingle, finding a partner.
4 Using only their outline, students talk about their readings with a partner.
5 The procedure is repeated with a second partner and with a third partner.
6 Students find a fourth partner, and re-tell the article. This time their partner holds the outline as they talk.
7 The partners re-tell the article to the original tellers using the outline to guide them.
8 In plenary, volunteers tell the class about interesting facts from readings reported to them.

Note

This is an excellent review activity. It works so well in large multilevel classes because students are permitted to repeat material to many different listeners. This invariably makes them add and embellish on the material. Steps 6, 7, and 8 also allow students to check their own comprehension and ability to summarize and talk about things they have read.

Box 20 Example of an outline

An outline works like this
I Main topic
    A. Secondary topic
        1. detail
           a. supporting detail
II Second main topic

Acknowledgement
This activity is a variation of one that I learned in a workshop given by my creative colleague Kevin Keating from the Center for English as a Second Language at the University of Arizona in Tucson, Arizona.

2.7 Friendship

Aim   fluency practice, class cohesion
Level   intermediate–advanced
Time   20–30 minutes

Procedure

1 Ask the class what qualities they look for in a good friend, and summarize their responses to single words that you write up on the board. If class volunteers haven't contributed enough responses, add some of your own. (See Box 21 for possible suggestions of qualities.)
2 Students rank the qualities in order of importance.
3 In small groups, students explain why they have ranked the qualities as they did.
4 In plenary, volunteers tell the class which quality they placed first and explain why.

Extension

For homework, students write short compositions about friendship or about a person that they consider to have been a good friend.

Box 21 Friendship qualities

- Loyal
- Tells the truth
- Is fun to be with
- Supports his/her friends
- Intelligent
- Sympathetic
- Understanding
- Likes me the way I am

2.8 More about friendship

Aim   fluency practice, class cohesion
Level   intermediate–advanced
Time   20–30 minutes

Procedure

1 Talk with the class about different kinds of friendships. Friendships
  come in all varieties. Some are much more intense than others.
  Some people we call friends we see only once a month or even once
  a year. Others we see every day. Elicit varieties of friendships from
  the class and add some yourself, and make a list on the board. (See
  Box 22 for possible suggestions of kinds of friends.)
2 Students copy the list and check three kinds of friendships that they
  have experienced.
3 In small groups, students talk about the people who have been their
  friends and why they value these friendships.
4 In plenary, volunteers talk about their friendships or about interesting friendships that they heard about in their group talk.

Box 22 Examples of kinds of friends

- Friends to shop with
- Friends to play tennis with
- Friends to talk to
- Friends to tell everything to
- Friends to spend lots of time with
- Friends to write to
- Friends that will listen to you
- Friends with whom to go to the movies
- Friends with whom to talk about books
- Friends with whom to hunt or fish

2.9 People I admire

Aim   fluency practice, class cohesion
Level intermediate–advanced
Time 20–30 minutes

Procedure

1 Together with your students, compose a list of people who are admired all over the world. (See Box 23 for possible suggestions.)
2 Students make their private list of people they admire.
3 Students stand and mingle.
4 They approach three classmates, one at a time, and tell each other whom they admire the most and why.
5 In plenary, volunteers tell the class about a personality that they had never heard of previously but who was admired by someone else in the class.

Note

Many students will choose to talk about a member of their family or their immediate friendship circle – this is to be encouraged, as it further contributes to class cohesion.

Extension

In class or at home, students can be encouraged to write about an admired person. Post their compositions on classroom walls to be read and commented on by classmates. *Allow only positive comments.*

Box 23 Admired people

Kemal Ataturk   Dr. Sun Yat-sen
The Prophet Mohammed   Dr. Jonas Salk
Albert Einstein   Dr. Martin Luther King
Mother Theresa   Queen Victoria
Princess Diana   Marie Curie
President Kennedy

2.10 Special places

Aim   fluency practice, class cohesion
Level intermediate–advanced
Time   20–30 minutes

Procedure

1 Dictate the following list:
  • Pride
  • Happiness
  • Loneliness
  • Self-fulfillment
  • Envy
  • Anger
  • Discovery
  • Fear
2 Make sure that all students understand the meanings of the words.
3 Next to each word students write a place where they experienced the feeling. The place may be a geographic entity like *New York City* or *Istanbul*. It can also just be a description of a place like *My grandmother's kitchen*.
4 Students stand and mingle.
5 They approach three classmates, one at a time, and tell each other about one of the places on their list. They describe how they felt and why.
6 In plenary, volunteers tell the class about something interesting that was reported to them by a conversation partner.

Extension

For homework, students write about *A special place*. Post the compositions on the walls of the classroom to be read and commented on by classmates. ***Allow only positive comments.***

2.11 Dreams I have

> **Aim**   fluency practice, class cohesion
> **Level** intermediate–advanced
> **Time** 20–30 minutes

Procedure

1 On the board or the overhead projector write:
   • A dream for myself
   • A dream for my family
   • A dream for my community
   • A dream for my country
   • A dream for the world
2 Together with the class define the concept *community*. (See Box 24 for suggestions.)
3 Share some of your own dreams with your class. (See Box 25 for suggestions.)
4 Students stand and mingle.
5 They approach three classmates, one at a time, and tell each other about their dreams. They explain why these dreams are important to them.
6 In plenary, volunteers tell the class about something interesting that was reported to them by a conversation partner.

Extension

This is an excellent pre-reading activity for Martin Luther King's famous speech: *I have a dream*.

Box 24 Definitions of community

- The place where you live
- Your religious group
- Your social group
- Your friendship circle
- People of your nationality
- People who share your beliefs

Box 25 Suggestions for personal dreams

- For myself: I want to write a novel
- For my family: I want us to travel in England together
- For my community: I want good and free medical care for everyone
- For my country: An excellent and free education for every person from kindergarten through to Ph.D.
- A dream for the world: Peace and prosperity

2.12 How I feel now

Aim	fluency practice, class cohesion
Level	intermediate–advanced
Time	15–20 minutes

Procedure

1 With the help of volunteers, make a list of adjectives that describe people. If the class does not suggest many, offer some of your own. (See Box 26 for suggestions.)
2 Students choose an adjective that best describes them at this particular moment.
3 Students stand up and mingle.
4 They approach three classmates, one at a time, and tell each other about which adjective they have chosen and why this adjective describes them well.
5 In plenary, volunteers tell the class about something interesting or amusing that was reported to them by a conversation partner.

6 In plenary, ask *How many students were tired?* Count hands and ask for individual reasons.
7 Continue the procedure with several other adjectives.

Extension

Students write about *How classrooms make me feel.* Post compositions on the classroom walls to be read and commented on by classmates.

Box 26 Suggested adjectives

- Happy
- Sleepy
- Tired
- Bored
- Excited

- Interested
- Smart
- Silly
- Rested
- Beautiful

2.13 Slip exchange

Aim	speaking, reading, exchanging opinions, review
Level	all levels
Time	fluid
Preparation	On slips of paper make out questions on the material you have just read, or on any topic that is under discussion, or possibly on the lives of students. (See Box 27 for suggestions.) Put all the slips in a bag.

Procedure

1 Students pick a slip from the bag.
2 Students mingle. They read their question to a partner who answers, and then asks his/her question.
3 Students exchange slips and move on to the next classmate.
4 Continue as long as interest is high.

Variation

Ask students to create the questions on slips of paper before the exchange begins.

Box 27 Examples of personal questions

- Have you seen any good movies lately? Please tell me about one.
- What kind of music do you like?
- Why are you studying English?
- What is your favorite city?
- What do you do when you want to relax?
- What do you like to read?
- What is your favorite food?
- What kinds of restaurants do you like?
- Do you have any hobbies?
- What is your favorite season?

2.14 Flip-flop books

Aim	organizing material, speaking, writing, review of content
Level	all levels
Time	fluid
Preparation	Bring enough pieces of construction paper to have one piece for each student and a few extra pieces. Bring a few pairs of scissors, one for each group of students.

Procedure

1 Students sit in groups of five; each student has a piece of construction paper.
2 Students fold their papers in half horizontally.
3 Students cut the top flap into four sections.
4 On each of the four flaps now created, students write an aspect of the topic you want to review. (See Box 28 for suggestions.)
5 Students lift the flap and on the top and bottom of each inside they write three sentences that summarize their topic.
6 Students show their flip-flop books to their group and read their sentences.
7 Each group of five chooses the most interesting flip-flop book to present to the whole class.

Note

Some artistic learners love to decorate their flip-flop books.

Variation

When the topic you have been discussing only has three main sections, students create only three flaps.

Box 28 Possible topics for flip-flop books

- Characters, setting, problem, solution
- The judicial, the executive, the legislative
- Cities, rivers, mountains, deserts
- Proteins, starches, fruits, vegetables
- Positive, negative, neutral
- Middle class, upper class, lower class
- Foods I like, foods I don't like, foods I should eat
- Summer, winter, fall, spring
- Oceans, rivers, lakes

2.15 **Frame it**

Aim   speaking, re-charging previous knowledge, organization
Level all levels
Time 20 minutes

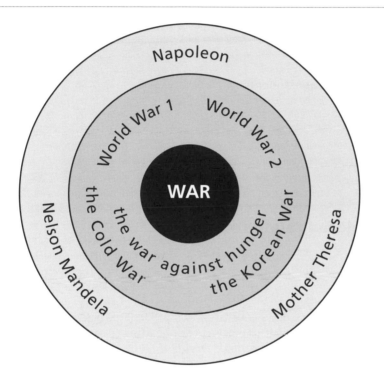

Procedure

1 Students write the topic or issue that you suggest in a circle in the middle of their paper. This becomes their central picture. (See Box 29 for suggestions.)
2 Around the circle, students write any words or associations that come to mind when they see the topic. This is the first frame of their picture.
3 Around the associations, students write the names of people who have influenced their thinking about this topic.
4 In small groups students explain their pictures.
5 Each group chooses its most interesting picture to present to the entire class.

> ## Box 29 Possible topics for framing
>
> **For advanced students**
> - War
> - Communication
> - Transportation
> - Pollution
> - Political figures
> - Hunger in the world
> - Old age
>
> **For beginner students**
> - Favorite foods
> - Favorite people
> - Best places
> - Home
> - A loved relative
> - Animals
>
> **For intermediate students**
> - Foods
> - Clothes
> - Houses
> - Faces
> - Shopping
> - Doctors

2.16 Colored round robin

Aim	writing, speaking, review
Level	all levels
Time	20–30 minutes

Preparation Post several pieces of large paper around the room. On each paper write as heading a topic that relates to what you have studied. Divide the class into groups and give each group a differently colored felt marker.

Procedure

1 In groups, students walk from poster to poster. They brainstorm ideas and choose a representative who writes down a summary of what they have said on the poster.
2 When all the groups have been to all the posters, read what has been written on the posters, and when you need clarification or want further explanation, the color in which something has been written will tell you which group to turn to.

Acknowledgement

This activity is a variation of one that I learned from my creative colleague and frequent co-author, Laurel Pollard.

2.17 Circle talk

Aim   fluency practice, class cohesion
Level all levels
Time   20 minutes

Procedure

1 Students form inner and outer circles of about eight students in each inner and each outer circle. Students facing outward form the inner circle and students facing inward form the outer circle, so that each student from the inner circle has a partner in the outer circle.
2 The inner circle students will not talk, but show their partners that they are good listeners. (See Box 30 for qualities of a good listener.)
3 Give the students a topic. (See Box 31 for suggested topics.)
4 Students in the outer circle have one minute to talk about the topic.
5 Students in the outer circle move one step to the right and face a new partner.
6 Students in the outer circle have two minutes to talk about the same topic.
7 Students in the outer circle again move one step to the right and face a new partner.
8 Students in the outer circle have three minutes to talk about the topic.
9 Repeat the entire procedure with the inner circle.

Extension

Students write about the topic.

Note

The activity is an excellent pre-reading activity for preview of the topic to be read about or as a post-reading activity for a topic already read about.

Box 30 Qualities of a good listener

A good listener:
- is attentive to what the speaker says
- does not allow his/her mind to wander
- doesn't interrupt
- looks at the speaker
- nods, smiles, and makes facial expressions of understanding
- re-phrases some of the speaker's statements to make sure he/she has understood
- is patient
- asks for repetition if something is not clear

Box 31 Circle talk topics

For advanced students
- Travel
- Prejudice in the world
- A book I loved
- The importance of money
- Equality for women
- Why the rich grow richer and the poor grow poorer
- How computers are changing the world
- What is important in a career

For intermediate students
- Learning a language
- The best kind of weekend
- Games I played as a child
- My neighborhood
- The kinds of clothes I like
- My favorite teacher

For beginner students
- My room
- My family
- What I do every morning
- My favorite place
- The kind of weather I like
- How to cook or bake something
- How to clean a house

2.18 Teaming up

Aim	fluency practice, class cohesion, review
Level	all levels
Time	fluid
Preparation	Write out a set of questions that you want to use for review or test preparation.

Procedure

1 Students sit in groups of five. Each student is assigned a number from one to five.
2 Each group gives itself a name.
3 A student secretary writes all the group names on the board.
4 Call out a question with a number from one to five.
5 Students in each group huddle and make sure that the student whose number is called knows the answer. That student raises his/her hand.
6 Call on the first group in which the correctly numbered student has raised a hand.
7 If the answer is correct, that group gets a point. If incorrect, call on another group.
8 Continue until all questions have been answered and declare a winning group.

2.19 Needle in a haystack

Aim	scanning for information, pre-reading
Level	all levels
Time	fluid
Preparation	Prepare a set of questions based on a reading that is available to students, but that they have not yet read. Make enough copies for all groups in your class.

Procedure

1 Students sit in small groups.
2 Each group receives a set of questions and is directed to the reading.

3 The first group that has all the answers calls out.
4 If the answers are correct, the group is declared winner and a spokesperson from the group explains the answers to the entire class.

Note

This exercise works very well for newspaper reading, when some of the questions can be based on headlines or on captions, and some on information inside articles or advertisements.

2.20 Optimistic snapshots

> **Aim**   fluency practice
> **Level** all levels
> **Time** fluid

Procedure

1 Tell students to imagine that you were following them around during the previous week with a camera, and you want them to think of a happy or interesting moment during the past week when you would have snapped a picture of them.
2 Give students a minute to think about this and to write some notes about their snapshot.
3 Students mingle telling at least three different classmates about their snapshot.
4 Students tell the whole class about one snapshot that they heard about.

2.21 Words on cards

> **Aim**   fluency practice, review, vocabulary study, sentence formations
> **Level**   all levels
> **Time**   fluid
> **Preparation** Prepare sets of index cards. Each set of five should have the same vocabulary item written on each card. Make enough cards so that there will be one card for each student.

Procedure

1 Shuffle the cards so that the sets are all mixed up in the deck.
2 Students draw a card each.
3 Students mingle until they have found all five classmates who have the same word.
4 In groups of five, students define their word and write as many sentences as possible that include their word until you stop them.
5 In plenary, students read their definitions and examples.

2.22 A solution for the problem

Aim	fluency, class cohesion, problem solving
Level	all levels
Time	10 minutes

Procedure

1 Students sit in pairs.
2 A tells B about some difficulty he/she has in language learning.
3 B offers a solution.
4 They switch.
5 Volunteers tell the entire class about the solutions they received.

2.23 Student-centered dictation

Aim	writing, speaking, clear pronunciation
Level	all levels
Time	fluid
Preparation	Think of some interesting topics that your class could have ideas about.

Procedure

1 Students divide a page into three columns. The columns are headed with the words *Agree*, *Disagree*, and *Not Sure*.
2 State the topic.
3 A volunteer suggests a sentence based on the topic.
4 Students write the suggested sentence in one of the three columns

depending on how they feel about the sentence.

5 Another volunteer offers a sentence and the process continues as long as there is interest.

6 Students mingle telling one another where they placed the sentences and why they placed them as they did.

7 In plenary, students talk about an interesting placement of a sentence that they heard about.

Extension

Students write a paragraph on the topic.

Notes

– This exercise can be used as either pre-reading or post-reading on a topic.

– For beginning students, you might want to have sentences ready on slips of paper for students to pull and read.

– The exercise is excellent for pronunciation because if students don't understand what a classmate dictates, they will ask for many repetitions and thus cause improvement in pronunciation.

2.24 The seminar

Aim	reading, discussion, question formation
Level	intermediate–advanced
Time	fluid
Preparation	Choose an interesting reading passage.

Procedure

1 Students read the assigned passage silently and underline or highlight anything that jumps out at them. (This may be something interesting or difficult or even confusing.)

2 Students look at what they have underlined and formulate questions about the underlined parts.

3 Each student writes one question on the board.

4 Together with the class, categorize the questions. (See Box 32 for suggestions of categories.)

5 In small groups, students discuss the questions and answer them.

6 Each group tells the entire class about what they consider their best answer.

Extension

Assign reading and summary of the passage at home.

Box 32 Suggestions of categories in questions

- Questions dealing with language
- Questions dealing with facts
- Questions dealing with emotions
- Questions it will be hard to answer
- Questions dealing with opinions
- Questions dealing with numbers
- Questions dealing with people

---

3   Reviewing while maintaining interest and momentum

Large multilevel classes come in many packages. Sometimes we teach short six to eight week courses, and meet our students every single day. At other times, we might meet our students only once a week. Some of us teach in settings where we meet our classes three or four times a week in school situations where English is only one subject among many. Occasionally, we are asked to teach classes that we simply haven't had time to prepare for. The block of time that faces us may seem huge and empty. Anxiety strikes, and we wonder what on earth we are going to do with all that time. Then, at other times, we are overwhelmed by the amount of material that we must cover in a short period and we find ourselves rushing through things that we know need a great deal of recycling and reinforcement. **Such recycling and reinforcement is particularly essential in the large multilevel class, where some students are racing ahead while others are in great need of meaningful review.** Our problem is to provide the kinds of activities that will offer the much needed review for those who need it, while keeping the more advanced learners involved and interested. We should stimulate the thinking of those who are less interested while stretching the thinking of those already well involved.

We will do both our students and ourselves a great favor if we don't rush and remember that we are teaching language and not necessarily covering material. In language learning, rather than covering territory, we uncover meaning and discover function. Learning a language means practicing a set of skills rather than mastering specific content. Language learning works better when we bring about a sense of seamlessness in which students add lesson to lesson and feel a sense of purpose through continuity. Such a sense of momentum is best created through recycling and reviewing activities that remind our students of what they have learned and prod them to add new knowledge to old knowledge through a communicative network. **In the large multilevel class, where a student can easily feel lost, such a sense of continuity helps to create the classroom community where our students will feel supported in their language progress.** A sense of continuity can be achieved if the form of activities remains the same while the content changes. The activities in this chapter are routines that can be used over and over again – each time with a different content. They can help us to maintain the momentum of language learning by giving us frameworks for our curriculum and vehicles for meaningful recycling.

3.1 Answers into questions

Aim	review, writing, composing questions
Materials	sticky tape cut up into pieces for easy access in some central place, like the edge of your desk
Level	all levels
Time	fluid

Preparation   Look over the three previous lessons you have taught and produce six to ten answers to questions. These can be sentences from a text you have read, examples of grammar points you have stressed, or vocabulary that you have introduced.

Procedure

1 Write the answers you have produced on the board, or project them on an overhead projector. Tell students that these are answers to questions on material they have studied.
2 Working in pairs, students write the questions that will elicit the answers you have written up. Circulate to help them with question formation. Each question should be written on a separate slip of paper.
3 Students choose their two best questions and using the sticky tape, stand and paste each question on the back of a classmate other than the partner they have been working with.

4 Students mingle. They read a question from the back of a partner out loud to this partner and that partner has to look on the board to find and provide the answer to the question.

5 The students switch roles. The one with the question on his/her back has to remember what was previously asked and ask it again, while the first student must provide the answer, this time without looking on the board.

6 Students move on to a new partner and repeat the procedure.

7 Continue the activity as long as there is high interest.

Note

This activity produces a lot of laughs, and much re-reading.

Optional follow-up

Students can write a brief summary of the material covered in the answers.

3.2 Review posters

Aim	review, writing, fluency practice, summarizing skills
Materials	large pieces of paper (possibly newsprint), tape, felt markers, glue or glue sticks, and if available, old magazines
Level	all levels
Time	45–60 minutes

Procedure

1 At the end of a unit or a section of a unit, work with the class to elicit the main points of the unit. Write these on the board or an overhead projector. Show students where papers, felt pens, tape, and old magazines are.

2 In groups of three, students produce a visual poster of the main ideas. This can be done through charts, questions, brief summaries or pictures.

3 Students post their finished work on the walls of the class.

4 Those who finish early join groups that are still working and help in the completion of the posters.

5 Each group appoints a spokesperson who stands next to the group poster and explains it to the entire class.

6 Posters are left up on the wall and are used for review purposes during several following lessons.

Note

In the following lessons, when the posters are used as review, I have asked students to talk about posters produced by classmates. If they misinterpret the poster, the group which produced it is, as a rule, happy to come to the rescue, thus creating a double step review. See illustration for sample poster on the topic of meal planning.

3.3　Student-made quickie quizzes

Aim　review, writing, class cohesion
Level　all levels
Time　15–20 minutes

Procedure

1 Talk with the class about how one goes about making up a short answer quiz. Explain that the questions have to be very clear and call for one to three word answers.
2 With the help of your class, create a few questions on material you have recently studied, and write these up on the board.
3 In groups of three, students create short answer quizzes. Each quiz should have no more than five questions, but groups that finish early can produce more and then choose their five best questions for use.

4 Decide on the formula for grading. For example, each correct answer can be worth 20 points.
5 Each group passes its quiz on to another group.
6 In groups, students take the quiz.
7 Finished quizzes are passed back to the original group that grades them following the agreed formula.
8 Graded quizzes are passed back to the group who took the quiz.
9 In plenary, talk about whether the grading was fair and what was difficult about making the quiz or taking the quiz.

Note

At the conclusion of this exercise, I have invariably received much appreciation for the work of a teacher who has to make out quizzes all the time!

3.4 Group reviews

Aim   review, summary, fluency practice, writing

Level   all levels

Time   20–30 minutes

Preparation   Make a set of questions on the material your class has studied.

Procedure

1 In small groups, students work through the questions. They are allowed to talk and to use their books. All the students in the group sign their names on the paper that is handed in.
2 Correct the papers, giving each a group grade, and allow groups to meet the following day to make appropriate corrections.
3 Tell them that the test that they will take individually and with closed books will have very similar and perhaps even some of the same questions.

Notes

– I tend to give such a group review as a midterm, and the individualized closed-book test as a final. I have found the procedure is greatly appreciated by students and helps to foster good study habits.
– One of the great advantages of the group review is that you will have only as many papers to correct as there are groups.
– Group size is anywhere between two and five. Students who prefer working alone should be allowed to do so.

3.5   Group summaries

Aim   review, writing, reading for meaning, fluency skills
Level   intermediate–advanced
Time   30–40 minutes

Procedure

1   Elicit and/or explain the meaning of the word *summary*.
2   In small groups, students talk about when and why one must occasionally summarize what one has read or heard. (See Box 33 for suggestions.)
3   Dictate: *A summary is … .*
4   Students finish the sentence in any way they wish.
5   Listen to several volunteers reading their sentences.
6   Together with the class, define and refine the definition of summary. The following main ideas should come across:
    • A summary is shorter than (about a third of) the original.
    • A summary does not state the writer's own opinions.
    • A summary includes the main ideas of the original.
7   In small groups, students study a passage that you have recently read in class. They locate the main ideas.
8   Listen to several suggestions and write a composite that seems most suitable on the board.
9   In small groups, students write a summary of the passage.
10 Several summaries are read out and rated on the three attributes in step 6.

Box 33 Suggestions for when one needs summaries

• When one wants to tell someone about a good movie one has seen.
• When one wants to tell someone about a good book one has read.
• When one needs to study something one has read.
• When one needs to remember something important.
• To talk about the main ideas of what happened in a meeting.
• To talk about the news.
• To describe an accident.
• To tell someone about a trip one has made.
• To talk in class about material one has read.
• To make a presentation in class or at a conference.

3.6   Vocabulary wall

Aim   review, vocabulary study
Level   all levels
Time   5–10 minutes each lesson

Procedure

1 Assign one part of a classroom wall to become the 'vocabulary wall'.
2 At the beginning of lessons, ask students if they heard any words that they didn't understand or if there were words in their text that they found particularly difficult.
3 One student takes on the responsibility to write these words in large clear letters – each word on a separate card or piece of paper.
4 Post the words on the vocabulary wall.
5 Spend some time each lesson reviewing the vocabulary wall – students should know how to pronounce a word, how to spell it, and how to use it in a sentence.
6 When everyone in the class is sure of the word, remove it from the vocabulary wall.

3.7   Class goals

Aim   class cohesion, fluency practice
Level   intermediate–advanced
Time   15–20 minutes

Procedure

1 At the beginning of the term, ask students to write down their personal goals in learning English during the session. (See Box 34 for suggested goals.)
2 In small groups, students talk about their goals and reach a consensus on one or two important goals.
3 Spokespersons from groups report on group goals. Write these on the board.
4 The class votes on the five most important goals for the whole class.
5 Post these goals on a large piece of paper in a conspicuous spot.

6 Periodically, review the goals with the class and ask students to talk, in groups, about their own progress.

Box 34 Suggested session goals

- To learn more words
- To become more fluent
- To improve my grade
- To improve my reading skills
- To improve my writing
- To make fewer mistakes
- To talk more to native speakers
- To read a whole book in English
- To write letters in English

3.8 The KWL procedure

Aim	introduction of a new topic, fluency practice, vocabulary review
Level	all levels
Time	20–30 minutes

Preparation On a large piece of paper, draw a three column chart. (See Box 35 for an example of a chart.) As a heading for the first column write the word *Know*. As a heading for the second column write the words *Want To Know*. As a heading for the third column write the word *Learned*.

Procedure

1 On the board, write the topic that you wish to introduce.
2 In small groups, students pool their knowledge of the topic.
3 A spokesperson for each group reports the group findings, while you or a student recorder summarizes the information and writes it in the *Know* column.
4 In small groups, students write questions that they have about the topic.
5 A spokesperson for each group reads out the questions while you or a student recorder summarizes the questions under the *Want To Know* heading.

6 Volunteers provide answers for any of the questions that have been posed and the recorder puts these under the *Learned* heading.
7 Tell the class that as you pursue the topic you will find answers to the remaining questions and perhaps much other interesting information.
8 As your study of the topic progresses, bring out the chart and complete the third column.

Box 35 Example of a KWL chart on bats

Know	Want To Know	Learned
They fly at night.	Are they like birds?	
They eat insects.	How can they fly if they are blind?	They have a radar system.
They are small.	Why are people afraid of them?	Because they are animals of darkness, and people think that frightening things happen at night. Also, many strange stories and superstitions have been made up about bats.
There are many stories about them.	How do you get a bat out of your house?	Light bothers them. So if you put the light on in your house at night and leave the door open, the bat will fly out.
They are blind.		

3.9   The Venn diagram

Aim	comparing and contrasting, fluency practice, review of topics that can be compared and/or contrasted
Level	all levels
Time	15–20 minutes
Preparation	Draw a large Venn diagram on the board.

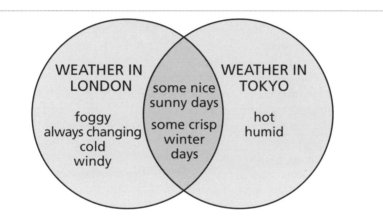

Procedure

1 From the topics that you have studied, choose two themes, ideas or things to be compared or contrasted. These should be concepts that have some overlap. (See Box 36 for suggestions.)
2 Write these two concepts above the two extreme sections of the Venn diagram.
3 Divide the class into small groups (three to five students in each).
4 Assign some groups one of the concepts and ask them to list its qualities.
5 Assign other groups the second concept and ask them to list its qualities.
6 Spokespersons from each group report to the whole class.
7 Summarize the ideas and place them in the proper compartments on the Venn diagram that you have drawn on the board.
8 Ask several students to read out both sides of the diagram.
9 Volunteers contribute similar qualities, and a class secretary writes these in the middle compartment of the Venn diagram.
10 For homework, students write a composition which compares and contrasts the two concepts.

Variation

A three-way Venn diagram works well for three topics such as three
cities, three countries, three machines, three ways of studying, three
famous people.

Note

The Venn diagram is a good review mechanism as well as an excellent
discussion starter.

Box 36 Concepts for Venn diagram

For beginner students
- The weather in two countries
- Physical characteristics of two people
- Foods eaten for breakfast in different places
- Clothes worn for different occasions
- Schedules for every day and for day of rest

For intermediate and/or advanced students
- How schools in two countries are different, or how elementary
  school is different from high school
- How two different governments are organized
- The difference between two cities or countries
- Different rules for being polite
- Different marriage and courtship customs
- Life in a one-family house versus life in an apartment
- Differences in funeral customs
- Differences in religious beliefs
- The difference of attitudes between older and younger
  generations
- The difference of attitudes between men and women

3.10 Judging people

Aim   review of a story, fluency practice
Level intermediate–advanced
Time 20–30 minutes

Procedure

1 Draw a five column chart on the board. Students draw this chart on their papers. See Box 37 for an example of a chart that uses the story of Cinderella.
2 Students volunteer adjectives that describe people while you write these on the board.
3 The class votes on its four favorite adjectives and you place these as headings on the four last columns of the chart.
4 In the first column, students write names of characters in the story they have studied.
5 Students rate the characters on a scale of 0–5.
6 Students stand and mingle. They explain to one another how they rated a character and why they rated him/her that way, and move on to another student to talk about a different character.
7 Continue as long as interest is high.

Note

This review can also be used for historical figures; cities; countries.

Box 37 Example of judging people chart

	Courageous	Kind	Generous	Nasty
Cinderella	3	5	3	0
Stepmother	5	0	0	5
Hunter	2	4	3	2
Stepsisters	5	0	0	4
King	0	2	2	3

3.11 Running dictation

Aim	review, preview, reading, writing, speaking, listening, pronunciation
Level	all levels
Time	fluid

Preparation Make enough copies of a passage that you want to review for your entire class. You can also choose a passage from the textbook that your class already uses.

Procedure

1 Students sit in three rows: readers at one end of the class; runners in the middle; writers at the other end.
2 Runners get up and approach the readers, who have the text. The readers read one sentence to the runners.
3 The runners run to the writers and dictate the sentence they have heard. And as quickly as possible return to the readers for the next sentence.
4 Continue until one group is finished with the whole passage, and declare that group winner.
5 Let the whole class check the original text to see how closely they followed it.

Variation

To make the technique more lively, occasionally during the process of dictation shout *Switch* and let students exchange roles (readers become runners; runners become writers).

Note

This activity generates much laughter and fun.

3.12 My sentence

Aim	review, speaking, listening
Level	all levels
Time	fluid
Preparation	Bring sticky tape to class.

Procedure

1 Students look over a reading they have recently studied and choose one sentence that somehow speaks to them – perhaps they completely agree with it or disagree with it or don't understand it or find it beautiful or perhaps it reminds them of something.
2 Students write their sentences on a piece of paper that they pin or tape to themselves.
3 Students mingle, reading the sentences of others and asking those they meet to explain the sentences they have chosen.
4 Students try to find those who have chosen the same sentence. They stand together and explain to one another why they have chosen the particular sentence.
5 In plenary, volunteers offer their sentences together with explanations.

3.13 Where is my other half?

Aim	review, speaking, listening, reading
Level	beginners
Time	10–20 minutes

Preparation   Choose some sentences from a reading passage you have recently done. Write them on slips of paper and cut each sentence in two halves. Have enough half sentences for your entire class (one half sentence for each student).

Procedure

1 Students stand and mingle. They read their half sentences to one another until they find the second half of their sentence.
2 All the sentences are read out.
3 Students form a line in the order of how the sentences appeared in the text.
4 Teacher reads the original text, and students re-arrange themselves to correct any mistakes in order.

3.14 Person, place or thing

Aim	speaking, categorizing, review
Level	beginners
Time	fluid

Preparation   Write a list of nouns in three categories – persons, places, or things. (See Box 38 for noun suggestions.) Copy the list, so that there is one list for each group of three students. Cut up the lists into slips, so that there is one word on each slip. Put each set of slips into an envelope, so that you have one envelope of nouns for each group of three students. Put an eraser in each envelope.

Procedure

1 In groups of three, students take turns pulling a slip out of the envelope.
2 They read the word and say whether it is a person, place, or thing.
3 If they get it right, they keep their slip and the game moves on to the next student.

4 If they get it wrong and another student catches them, that student has to grab the eraser and make the correction.
5 The student who made the mistake must put all his/her slips back in the envelope. (There will be some argument, which is just fine for language use and you might have to be the final arbiter.)
6 Continue the game as long as there is high interest. Then review all the objects with the entire class.

Variation

The game can be used with any set of categories. Examples: *rivers, cities, countries; complete sentences, fragments, run ons; verbs, adjectives, adverbs; clothes, food, toys; animals, vegetables, inanimate objects.*

Suggestion

Ask a student in each group to collect the slips when the game is over so that you can use them again without having to go through the cutting up procedure. I have also asked students to create the original list and do their own cutting.

Box 38 Noun suggestions

Chair, table, store, city, mountain, bread, fruit, postman, brother, mother, apple, book, baby, printer, pencil, father, cousin, sock, sugar, home, lake.

---

4   Dealing with written work

Learning how to write is important

Our students who all live in today's literate world need to learn how to write for very practical reasons. Newcomers to a country soon have to start communicating through writing. They have to write notes to a child's teacher. They have to take down telephone messages. They have to fill out job applications and applications for health insurance. Sometimes they have to leave a note for the mailman or write a thank-you letter. Students in school at all stages of the academic ladder need to express themselves in writing to do well in school.

Writing is a valuable skill for many other reasons as well. Lonely people find a companion in their diaries. Writing reinforces spoken language, and many people claim that writing helps them to think. There are language learners who say that they cannot possibly learn a word unless they write it down. Some people cannot make a decision unless they sit down and write the pros and cons of each side. Through sentence writing, students reinforce grammatical structures, as well as vocabulary.

Teaching writing is not easy

Literacy, unlike talking, is not a natural skill. We must remember that humanity existed for centuries in highly communicative and linguistically sophisticated societies that were largely illiterate. Reading and writing are social inventions that have to be taught and learned, practiced and mastered.

Learning to read and write is particularly difficult for students who come from writing systems that are different than those of the target language. These students must struggle just to learn forming the letters before they can dream of communicating through literacy.

Teachers of large multilevel classes often complain that writing is the most problematic skill to teach in such classes. Writing, indeed, does seem the most challenging of the four skills to master. Many very fine and caring teachers have told me that they have simply given up on writing. 'In the huge classes I teach, I just cannot read and comment on everything students write, and if they don't get feedback on their writing, they don't write,' said one very discouraged and very conscientious teacher.

To complicate things, many good language learners panic when they have to write. My good friend, Dawn, for example, is very articulate and can tell wonderful stories – using just the right words, metaphors, and symbols when she talks. However, when she has to write the simplest things, her perfectionist bug bites bringing with it a severe case of writing anxiety and Dawn freezes.

Some of the difficulties can be overcome

In spite of everything you have read and heard, writing is just talking on paper or on the computer screen – just that, talking on paper. I can hear you protesting. Intuitively, you know that spoken language is much more spontaneous than written language. You realize too that in writing we don't get all the visual suggestions of gestures and facial expressions, or the phonic clues of voice level and tone that give us hints of meaning. You know that speech is much more repetitive and circuitous than writing. Nevertheless, I will insist that the best way of getting things down on paper or on the computer screen is to think of writing as just talking to someone who, at that particular moment, doesn't happen to be sitting right next to you. That, as far as I know, is the best way to get rid of the most troubling aspect of writing – the phenomenon of writing anxiety.

Practice makes perfect

Both reading and writing demand a lot of practice. Our students need to become comfortable with writing. To reach that level of comfort, they have to write a great deal. **As a matter of fact, they have to write every day and in every lesson, and in our classes, we can, if we plan correctly, give them that opportunity.**

Writing together with other skills

Writing is needed not only for its own value, but also for its ability to help us in recycling and internalizing all four skills. Writing ought to be combined with the other skills – listening, speaking, reading and thinking. Speaking and reading about a topic helps our students to rethink and formulate their ideas, get new ideas from other students and gather vocabulary that will be used in their writing. Conversely, getting some ideas down on paper is helpful as a prelude to speaking. Activities 4.1 and 4.4 are examples of how other skills are combined with writing.

Giving meaningful feedback

If it is really both difficult and important for students to write every day, then how do we go about giving students meaningful feedback? We know that when people talk, they hope that someone is listening. By the same token, when people write, they want someone to read what they have written. They write to communicate with someone – even when that someone turns out to be an older and perhaps wiser self. **However, the reader of student-produced texts need not necessarily always be the teacher.** Students who have been properly trained make excellent peer editors. Remember that writing will flow much more smoothly without the threat of the red pen hanging over it. Writing can mean re-writing – it doesn't always mean re-writing. As a matter of fact, some writing needs no feedback at all! (See activity 4.1 in this chapter.)

The computer has turned writing into a truly communicative activity, where feedback is an integral part of communication. On email, in cyberspace chat rooms, on web-sites, and in interactive classrooms all over the globe, people are saying things to one another in writing. People are automatically and effortlessly making corrections in their correspondents' spelling and grammar. They do so naturally, and in the best of pedagogical style, by simply repeating a word using its correct form. (See activities 4.6, 4.8, and 4.9 in this chapter.)

Some practical tips

- I keep a box with hanging folders in it, and I label each folder with the headings of the day. They may be: Group work, homework, or 'bell work' (quiet work that students do at the beginning of a lesson). When they finish their assigned written work, students simply deposit it in the right folder. It saves a great deal of paper confusion.
- I start each lesson with some written bell work. This assignment is always written on a certain part of the board, and students know where to find it. This gives everyone something to do right away and settles the class down.

- I give each student a number, which they learn to put next to their names. The numbers correspond to those in my attendance list. This way a student can quickly organize a stack of papers for me.
- I put each student's name and number on a wooden clothes peg, and place these around a large paper plate. The plate is visible to the whole class and if I remove his/her peg, a student knows that he/she owes me some written work, and that the peg will be replaced as soon as I get it. (This also reminds me that I must speak with the student whose peg is missing.)
- I insist that each composition go through a self-editing and two peer edits before it goes to me. (See activities 4.2 and 4.15.)
- I ask students to keep daily assignments in a notebook and I pick up two or three notebooks each day for check and/or correction. Students don't know whose notebook will be chosen on any given day. I collect some notebooks more than once to ensure that students know that their work can be looked at again even if they have already been pegged once.
- As I check daily homework, I walk around the room picking up notebooks here and there for a brief glimpse.
- I provide different colored paper for different drafts on which students work, for example, green paper for first drafts, yellow for second, and white for final drafts. That way, when I circulate in class, I can immediately see who is doing what and, as a result, give more meaningful help.

4.1 Keep it going

Aim	writing, reading, interpreting, reacting, sharing opinions
Level	intermediate–advanced
Time	30–40 minutes
Preparation	Students should have an interesting piece of writing – perhaps an article that you have already read and discussed.

Procedure

1 Students read the article either silently or in pairs – reading out loud one paragraph each.
2 Students underline the section/s that in some way interested them – they may have agreed with it, disagreed, been provoked by it, liked it, or perhaps it reminded them of something.

3 On loose pieces of paper, students write their names and their reaction to the section/s they have underlined (five to seven minutes writing time).

4 Students pass their paper together with the original text to another student.

5 Students read the paper they have received and add their own reaction to the comments.

6 Students pass the paper they have received to another student and the process is repeated.

7 Students again pass the paper and the process is repeated.

8 Students pass the papers back to the original owner who reads all the comments written.

9 In small groups, students talk about the comments on their papers and whether or not they agreed with the writers who added on to their papers.

10 In plenary, volunteers comment on how they felt about the whole process. Did it add to their comprehension of the article? Did they gain any new ideas?

4.2   Peer reviews

Aim	writing, listening, reading
Level	all levels
Time	30–45 minutes

Preparation   Prepare a Peer Review Form. (See Box 39 for an example.) Make, or ask students to make, two copies of their compositions. They then each have three copies of their compositions.

Procedure

1 In groups of three, students give each group member a copy of their composition.

2 From a central place in the room, each group takes nine review sheets.

3 Explain the difference between being a Reviewer (who reads for content) and an Editor (who reads for structure).

4 The first student in each group reads his/her composition out loud while his/her groupmates follow along. They can ask questions or make comments during the reading.

5 At the completion of the reading, each student fills out the reviewer/editor form.

6 The process is repeated with each student.
7 Students receive their peer review/edit forms and read the comments of classmates. They may wish to ask questions for clarification.
8 Students re-write compositions making appropriate additions and changes.
9 The compositions are filed in the cumulative folder. (See activity 4.15.)

Note

As an alternative to providing the reviewer/editor forms, you can simply write the information on the board and ask students to copy it on a piece of paper.

Box 39 Peer review form

Today's date ....

Writer's name ....

Reviewer's/editor's name ....

The reviewer

One thing that I liked in ....'s paper was

....

I also liked ....

My questions about the paper are: ....

I didn't understand ....

I would like more ....

....

The editor

I think that the writer should correct ....

....

© Cambridge University Press 2001

4.3   **Writing conferences**

Aim	writing, fluency practice, discussion, class to class communication
Level	intermediate–advanced
Time	fluid

Preparation   Ask students to choose the best composition from their composition folder and give these to you (see activity 4.15). Choose four compositions. These students will present their work at the writing conference.

Procedure

1 The four presenters present their compositions to the class. They should not just read aloud (though they may read parts from their compositions) but rather present their compositions through lecture format. If there is an overhead projector, they could use it, or they could provide an outline of their composition to each classmate or write the outline on the board.
2 After each presentation, allow some time for students to write questions or comments that relate to the composition.
3 Volunteers offer their questions and comments as you or an appointed student monitor lead the discussion.
4 When the discussion winds down or when you feel that enough time has elapsed, introduce the next speaker and repeat the procedure.

A more formal variation

1 Choose four compositions. The authors of these compositions will present their work at the writing conference. The presenters write brief biographies on cards. These cards will be used to introduce them at the conference.
2 Set a date for the conference.
3 Appoint a conference moderator, who will introduce the speakers and time the presentations.
4 Invite students from other classes.
5 On the day of the conference, the four presenters sit in front of the room.
6 Appoint four first reactors. Their job will be to summarize each presentation immediately after it has been given, and to ask a question or offer a first comment.

7 The moderator introduces each reader/speaker before they stand to read and speak. He/she times the speakers and signals them to end their presentation at the agreed time.

8 Readers stand and deliver their composition. They can read parts and talk their way through sections. (An overhead projector here is very helpful.)

9 After each presentation, the moderator invites the first reactor for a summary and a comment or a question.

10 The moderator continues to lead the discussion and stops it after the agreed time in order to introduce the next presenter.

11 The procedure is repeated for each presenter.

12 If the class has written on one general topic, a general discussion led by either the moderator or the teacher may follow.

Notes

– If possible, serve refreshments at the conclusion of the conference.
– Although the formal variation of the conference takes some time to prepare, it is usually an extremely successful event, and it creates a fine forum in which students share their writing with an interested audience.
– The activity works particularly well if two parallel classes work together on the conference.
– You may use any topics students choose from their compositions for the conference, or you might assign a general broad essay topic to be used for the conference. (For suggestions see Box 40.)

Box 40 Suggestions for topics that work well in a writing conference

- A challenge in my life
- What my culture can offer the world
- A change I would like to see in my country
- Improving our world
- The changing role of family in today's world
- How technology will change our lives
- Things we can look forward to

4.4   Write before you talk

Aim   writing, speaking
Level   intermediate–advanced
Time   10–15 minutes

Procedure

1 Ask a *why* question. See Box 41 for suggestions, and invite students to think of other *why* questions.
2 Allow students to write as much as they can on the topic of their choice. They need not write in complete sentences.
3 Circulate, helping out with vocabulary.
4 In small groups students discuss their topic and add comments to what they have written as they hear new ideas from classmates.
5 The discussion continues in plenary as each group makes contributions.
6 For homework, students can develop their ideas and later post their completed compositions on the walls of the classroom, so that classmates can read and comment on the work.

Note

You will find that a discussion preceded by such written prompts becomes rich and interesting. See Chapter two for other suggestions on talk that can lead to writing.

Box 41 Suggestions for *why* questions

- Why have there always been wars?
- Why are some animals disappearing?
- Why are people having fewer children?
- Why do people need to study foreign languages?
- Why do so many people travel?
- Why do women live longer than men?
- Why do married men live longer than single men?
- Why do some people hate living in cities?
- Why do some people love living in cities?
- Why are some people vegetarians?
- Why isn't everyone a vegetarian?

4.5 Buddy journals

Aim	writing, getting to know other students
Level	intermediate–advanced
Time	10–15 minutes

Preparation Make arrangements with another teacher whose class will participate with yours in the project. Make sure that there is a buddy for each of your students in the other class. Get the names of the students in the other class and put the names on strips of paper. Specify a day in the week which will be journal exchange day.

Procedure

1 Ask each student to supply a notebook for the buddy journal.
2 Students draw names of buddies.
3 On the assigned day, give students ten to fifteen minutes to write in the journals. Encourage them to introduce themselves and to ask questions about their buddies.
4 Exchange journals with your colleague.
5 Students answer the letters they received from their buddies in the other class.
6 When journals are returned, there will be a letter from the buddy from the other class in them.
7 Continue the procedure once a week on the designed day.
8 Occasionally ask students to comment on how they feel about the project. The reactions are usually positive.
9 At the end of the session have a 'buddy party' where students meet buddies and talk about their journals.

Notes

– Occasionally, students will be stuck and not know what to write about in their journals. For such occasions it is good to have a list of topics ready. (See Box 42 for suggested topics.)
– I have done these buddy journals between two schools as well as on email between two states and two countries. (See next activity on email journals.)

Box 42 Suggested topics for buddy journals

- My family
- Animals in my life
- What I like to do in my free time
- Films I have enjoyed
- Someone I admire
- My favorite relative
- How I feel about music
- How I feel about what is happening in the world today
- Sports
- Things, ideas, and people that are important to me
- My hobbies
- My hopes for the future
- Something I believe in

4.6   Using email

Aim	writing, exchange of ideas and information
Level	intermediate–advanced
Time	fluid

Preparation   If necessary, teach students how to use email; establish contact with a teacher in another community that also has access to email. Get your colleague's list of students and make sure that there are enough students to find a partner for each of yours. Ask your colleague to provide a picture and a brief description of each of her/his students and do the same for him/her. If you are teaching in a non-English speaking country, this can be a great way to correspond either with students from an English speaking one or students who speak a language different from the one of your country and thus use English as the common language.

Procedure

1 Assign your students an email partner. Try to match interests.
2 Students will correspond three times a week, and once a week send you a brief summary of the topics and/or ideas covered.

Extension

1 Students sit in small groups. When the chat room discussion is over, each group chooses a folder to read and comment on.
2 In their groups, students take turns reading out loud from the discussion and deciding which comments they find most interesting and most relevant.
3 A spokesperson from each group reports to the whole class.

Variation

Chat rooms with topics are posted on all the major search engines. If your class has access to computers, encourage students to use these.

Box 44 Suggestions for chat room discussion

- What is the best kind of government?
- Why adopting children is a blessing.
- Why it is better to marry later.
- Education is more important than I.Q.
- We must strive toward multi-cultural societies.
- Individualism is the most important of all values.
- Family is more important than society.
- Everyone thinks that their own culture is best.
- How can we lower the accident rate?
- What can be done to eliminate the drug problem?
- Everybody cheats on tests.
- There will always be a generation gap.
(Refer back to Box 31 for more ideas.)

4.9   Using web-sites

Aim   writing, publicizing student work
Level   all levels
Time   fluid
Preparation Create your own web-site.

Procedure

1 Each week choose a particularly interesting piece of student writing.
2 Invite the student you have chosen for an editing session, and

together with the student, edit the paper.

3 Publish the paper on your web-site and invite students to check in and write your email comments and reactions to the composition.

Notes

− This kind of publicity allows the students' friends and family all over the world to read their work.
− Encourage your students to build their own web-sites and to publish their own work.
− Teachers have a responsibility for child protection, so it is advisable to consider carefully the kind of personal information published, especially when working with younger learners.

4.10 **Writing about landscape pictures**

Aim	writing, reading, sharing ideas, learning about one another
Level	intermediate–advanced
Time	45–90 minutes
Preparation	Collect a set of pictures of landscapes or of cityscapes – preferably pictures without people. (*National Geographic Magazine* is a good source.) There should be at least one picture for each member of your class – the more pictures the better.

Procedure

1 Place pictures in a visible place.
2 Students choose pictures that remind them of something.
3 Students take their chosen pictures back to their desks and try to recollect as much as they can about the memory.
4 Collect the pictures.
5 Students write about their memory – not about the picture.
6 While the students are writing, post the chosen pictures around the walls.
7 Students bring their compositions to a centrally assigned place and pick up the composition of another student.
8 Students walk around the room looking at pictures and matching picture with composition. If they think they have found the right picture, they post the composition next to the picture.
9 Students stand next to their own picture. They see if the composition is the correct one. If it isn't they walk around the room

looking for their own composition and some exchanges are made.
10 Students tell the classmate standing next to them about their memory and how the picture was connected to it.

4.11 Writing about pictures of people 1

Aim   writing, sharing ideas

Level   beginners

Time   20–30 minutes

Preparation Have a set of pictures of people – at least one picture for each of your students – the more the better.

Procedure

1 From the selection of pictures each student chooses one.
2 Each student gets out a blank piece of paper.
3 Give students some time to study their picture and to think of a name for their person.
4 Students sit in groups of five.
5 Dictate the following: *This is ...*
6 Students write and fill in the name they have chosen.
7 Students pass the picture and the paper on to the person sitting next to them.
8 Dictate: *He/She lives in ...*
9 Students write on the paper they have received, basing the information on their impression of the second picture.
10 Dictate: *He/She lives with ...*
11 Students pass the picture and the paper on to the person sitting next to them. Dictate: *Yesterday was ... 's birthday.*
12 The procedure is repeated as above.
13 Dictate: *... is ... years old.*
14 The procedure is repeated as above.
15 Dictate: *All ... really wants for his/her birthday is ... .*
16 The papers and pictures by now should have returned to the original writers.
17 In their groups, students read their stories out loud to the group.
18 The group chooses its most interesting story. A spokesperson for the group goes to the front of the class and reads the group's story to the whole class, while another student holds up the picture. (See Box 45 for further suggestions.)

Box 45 Additional stem sentences

... hates
... loves
... admires
... wants to spend his/her vacation at ...
... dreams about ...
... knows a lot about ...
... is afraid of ...
... loves to eat ...
... is interested in ...

4.12 Writing about pictures of people 2

Aim　　　　writing, fluency practice
Level　　　intermediate–advanced
Time　　　30–40 minutes
Preparation　Have a set of pictures of people – at least one picture for each of your students – the more the better.

Procedure

1 From the selection of pictures each student chooses one.
2 Tell students to make up a name of the person they have chosen, an age, a place where the person lives, and something interesting, surprising or disappointing that has recently happened to the person.
3 Give them ten to fifteen minutes to write their stories.
4 In groups of five students hold up their pictures for the group to see and read their stories.
5 The group chooses the most interesting story.
6 A spokesperson for the group goes to the front of the class and reads the group's story to the whole class, while another student holds up the picture.

4.13 Service writing

Aim   writing, providing a service to the community

Level   advanced

Time   fluid

Preparation Call up a senior citizens' home and ask to speak
to their social director. Explain that you are teaching
ESL/EFL writing and that you are interested in providing
meaningful writing experiences for your students. Ask if
your students could be allowed to interview residents and
write their biographies.

Procedure

1 Talk with your students about what a biography is and explain why
   the project will benefit both them and their subjects. (See Box 46
   for suggestions.)
2 Students go to the senior citizens' home, and are introduced to
   their subjects. They spend several sessions talking with their
   subjects. They will want to use tape-recorders to capture what is
   being said.
3 Students write the biographies.
4 The subjects of the biographies read, add changes and correct.
5 Ask a group of colleagues to help you edit the projects.
6 Display sections of the biographies in a prominent display area.

Box 46 Reasons why the project will be a benefit

- Students will have a chance to meet new people and hear
  interesting life stories.
- Students will be able to practice real language to communicate
  about real life events.
- Students will learn about how life has changed.
- Students will learn about life in the community.
- Those who are interviewed will be able to share their life
  experience.
- Their life experience will become more meaningful through
  publication.
- Real friendships between generations can develop.

Notes

– The home may choose to publish the biographies.
– Make sure that your students have an introductory session with the social director of the institution to become familiar with the social ambiance and mores of the place.
– Service writing can also be done for other social institutions such as churches, mosques and synagogues, which need to compose advertisements, notices and/or brochures.
– As outlined above, the activity works best in ESL settings. In EFL settings, I have asked students to do this in the native language and to translate sections into English.

Follow-up tip

Some students become so impressed with the story of the life of their subjects that they begin writing their own autobiographies. You can encourage these efforts by focusing your students on topics such as:
• my life as a student
• my life as a son/daughter
• my life as a parent
• my life as a rebel
• my life as a believer
• my life as a dieter

4.14 A bio-poem class book

Aim	personal writing, getting to know fellow students
Level	all levels
Time	45–60 minutes
Preparation	Write your own bio-poem and be ready to share it with the class.

Procedure

1 Together with the class, compose and write on the board a bio-poem of a famous person.
  Here is the formula for a bio-poem:
  Line one: First name of person
  Line two: Three adjectives that describe that person
  Line three: Three *ing* verbs that suit the person
  Line four: Relative of ...
  Line five: Who loves ...

Line six: Who needs ...
Line seven: Who wants ...
Line eight: Who dislikes ...
Line nine: Who used to ...
Line ten: But above all, who ...
Line eleven: Resident of ...
Line twelve: One complete sentence describing person.
Line thirteen: Last name of person

(See Box 47 for an example of a bio-poem.)

2 Read your own bio-poem to the class.
3 In pairs, students interview partners and write bio-poems about them.
4 Post the bio-poems on the walls of your class.
5 Make a class book of bio-poems.
6 If possible, provide a book of bio-poems for each student and let students write messages to one another on the page where their bio-poem appears.

Note
This activity works very well as a capstone project for a writing class.

Box 47 Example of bio-poem

Snow White
Beautiful, beloved, lost
Cleaning, running, singing
Relative of a wicked queen
Who loves to eat apples
Who needs a prince to save her
Who wants to take care of the dwarves
Who dislikes dirt
Who used to live in a castle
But above all, who is very good.
Resident of the dwarves' cottage
She is such a good girl.
The Princess.

4.15 The cumulative folder

Aim	writing, self-correction
Level	all levels
Time	fluid
Preparation	Provide a folder for each student.

Procedure

1 Students keep all their writing in the folder.
2 On one side of the folder, students write the rules of grammar that they feel they have already mastered. (See Box 48 for examples.)
3 When you explain a new rule and students say that they understand it and are sure of it, they enter it on the list on the side of the folder.
4 Before handing in any written work, students check their folder list to see that they have followed these rules.
5 At the end of the session, students choose the best examples of their work and hand these in inside the folder.
6 Periodically, pick up a student folder and check one or two compositions for just the use of one or two of the rules.

Note

The folder serves as an excellent self-checking device.

Acknowledgement

I learned this activity from my talented colleague and frequent co-author, Laurel Pollard.

Box 48 Examples of rules

I know that a complete sentence has a subject and a verb.
I know that there is an *s* after a verb in the 3rd person singular, present tense.
I know that I have to put a period at the end of a sentence.
I know that a comma goes before the *and* in a compound sentence.

4.16 Sentences into story

Aim	writing
Level	all levels
Time	20–30 minutes
Preparation	Prepare five or six random sentences. (See Box 49 for examples.)

Procedure

1 Write the sentences on the board in any order.
2 In small groups, students turn the sentences into a story, by adding sentences, supplying names, and providing an ending for the story.
3 Each group reads its story.
4 The class votes on the most interesting story (nobody is allowed to vote on their own) and the whole class re-writes the chosen story by adding more details and making it more interesting.

4.17 Personalized guide books

Aim	writing, research
Level	intermediate–advanced
Time	fluid
Preparation	Write a guide book section of something interesting in the place where you were born, and be prepared to share this with your class. Bring guide books to class to show your students.

Procedure

1 Tell your class about the place where you were born and read some guide book samples. (See Box 50 for an example entry in the personalized guide book.)
2 In small groups, students tell one another about the place where they were born.
3 Students study the style of guide books.
4 Students research the place where they were born and write about a place visitors there might want to see.

Box 49 Examples of sentences

For beginners

I

He was hungry.
He had no money.
The old lady was nice.
The lady was friendly.
She had pretty eyes.
She cooked good soup.
He liked the soup.
There was meat in the soup.
They are good friends.

II

Her mother wasn't looking.
Annie walked out.
Annie was lost.
Annie cried.
Annie saw a policeman.
The police officer bought her
    ice-cream.
The police officer asked many
    questions.
Annie's mother was crying.
Annie and her mother hugged.
They thanked the police officer.

For intermediate students

I

It rained.
She made hot chocolate.
The cat came in.
The cat jumped into her lap.
She heard a sound.
She was afraid.
She recognized him.

II

Steven cheated on an exam.
Steven made a good grade on the
    exam.
His mother was surprised.
His father gave him some money.
He decided to tell the truth.
He told the teacher.
He told his parents.

For advanced students

I

I don't believe in ghosts.
I changed my mind.
He was as tall as a building.
His eyes were like burning fires.
I was terrified.
He spoke kindly.
He understood my problem.
I was no longer afraid.
He disappeared.

II

I lost all my money on a bad
    investment.
I lost all my friends.
My girl friend left me.
I was terribly depressed.
A letter came.
I went to a new country and found
    the work I had always wanted
    to do.
I made new friends.
Sometimes the worst things turn
    into the best things.
Life is full of surprises.

Extension
Make a class guide book for students to take home.

Box 50 Sample from personalized guide book

I was born in Yuma, Arizona, a small town on the Mexican
border. Many people in Yuma speak both English and Spanish.
It is very hot in Yuma in the summer, but in the winter the
weather is lovely and many visitors from the north come to
spend the winter. The place I like best in Yuma is a small
restaurant in the downtown area. The name of this restaurant is
The Garden. And it is really a beautiful garden full of trees and
flowers and birds that sing. The guests sit at little round tables
under the trees. *The Garden* has very good salads and desserts.
I love going there. If you come to Yuma, I hope you go to *The
Garden* for lunch.

4.18 Change the audience

Aim	studying different styles of writing
Level	advanced
Time	fluid

Preparation Bring several samples of writing to class. For
example: extracts from a newspaper, a novel, a magazine, a
children's book to read to your class.

Procedure

1 Read each sample out loud and ask students to notice the
differences.
2 In small groups, students look for more differences.
3 Read the first paragraph of a newspaper article and note how the
questions *when, where, who, how,* and *why* have been answered.
(See Box 51 for examples of articles and stories.)
4 In small groups, students re-write the article as if they were writing
it for a children's book.
5 Groups read their stories and the class comments on how each
differs from the newspaper article.

Variation

Students could re-write a children's story into a newspaper article, or turn part of a story into an advertisement, or a missing person's notice.

Box 51 Samples of genres that can be switched

The newspaper article
A new white-handed gibbon monkey was born last Monday at the Reid Park Zoo in Phoenix. It is a male. The mother's six previous offspring were all females. The white-handed gibbon is an endangered species animal.

The children's story
Last Monday everyone at the Reid Park Zoo was very happy and excited.
'It happened! It happened!' Mr Smith shouted when he came home for lunch.
'What happened, dear?' Mrs Smith asked.
'You'll never guess,' Mr Smith said.
'You got a new elephant?' said Mrs Smith.
'No, no!' Mr Smith shouted. 'It's Elsa, the gibbon. She had a baby! A baby boy!'

A novel
Sam and Betty were returning from a two-week vacation. They should have been refreshed but both of them were tired. They had both worked mightily at trying to save their marriage, and the effort had worn them out.

The diaries
From Sam's diary:
I love her so much. Walking on this beach with her again was a dream. If it would only last for ever. I think that I planned this perfectly. It was a lot of work but well worth it. Let's just hope that the romance can continue at home.

From Betty's diary:
Nothing has changed. He is as boring and predictable as ever. When I first met him I thought that he was so profound because he was always quiet. Now I have discovered that he doesn't talk because he has nothing to say.

4.19 **Clustering**

Aim   writing, gathering ideas, fluency practice
Level all levels
Time 30–40 minutes

Procedure

1 Choose a topic with which the entire class is familiar. (See Box 52 for suggested topics.)
2 Write the chosen topic in a circle in the middle of the board.
3 Draw branches from the topic out to subsidiary circles.

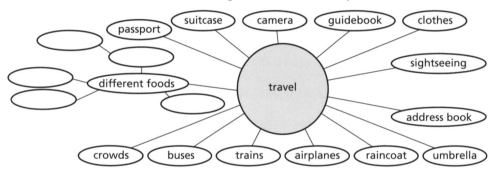

4 Volunteers provide sub-topics.
5 Choose one of the sub-topics to branch out from and continue the procedure as above.
6 In small groups, students choose another topic and do their own clustering.
7 Spokespersons from the group report on the clustering.
8 The class chooses one of the topics to write about.
9 Individually, students write the first paragraph of their compositions.
10 In small groups, students read out their paragraphs and receive suggestions on how to improve their paragraph and how to continue the composition.
11 Students complete the first draft of the composition at home.

Notes

Students may include all the topics they have clustered in their composition or only a few of these. One good way of organizing a composition is to have students finish the ideas in one cluster before they move on to another one.

Box 52 Suggested clustering topics

- Our school
- Our city
- An admired personality
- Healthy eating
- The dangers of smoking
- Having a pet

- Headaches
- Education
- Language learning
- Shopping
- Cars
- Sports

4.20 The writing cycle

Aim   writing, organization
Level   all levels
Time   fluid

Procedure

1 Explain that following certain procedures in writing can help us to organize our writing, although we need not always follow the steps in the order described here. (See Box 53 for suggestions.)
2 Ask for suggestions on how one gathers ideas before writing and put these on the board. (See activity 4.19.)
3 Continue as above with all the other stages in the box.
4 Choose a topic suggested by students and begin the process-writing cycle. Stop at the end of the lesson and ask students to complete the cycle up to the first draft at home.

Notes

- It is important that students understand the difference between 'drafting' and 'fine-tune editing'. When we draft we are concerned with content, ideas, and organization. When we fine-tune edit, we think more about mechanics.
- Following through on all the stages will improve student writing and eliminate a great deal of teacher correction.

Box 53 Suggestions for each of the seven process-writing stages

Pre-writing: clustering, brainstorming, talking to people, reading, listening to music

First attempts: writing sentences, writing phrases, writing the first paragraph, writing down any thoughts that come into your head

First draft: organizing and writing the composition as it seems best to you at this point

Reading for reactions: reading it out loud to yourself, to friends or family, to classmates, to the teacher, reading it – taping it – and listening to it

Organization: what should be the order of paragraphs, sentences, ideas

Re-drafting: writing the composition again incorporating new ideas (can be done several times)

Editing: reading the composition carefully to correct style, grammar, spelling, and punctuation

---

4.21 A resource for self-correction

Aim accuracy in writing

Level all levels

Time fluid

Preparation From any writing handbook or grammar book that you like, choose ten of the writing rules you feel that your class needs the most. Periodically check the list and if you feel that your students have mastered any of the rules on the list, add and/or make changes. After each rule, write an example. Base the examples on the lives of the students in your class. (See Box 54 for a suggested list.) Make several copies of the list.

Procedure

1 Post the rules lists in several places.
2 After completing a piece of writing, students take it up to one of the lists to check their composition.

3 As students write, circulate, checking their writing.
4 On a 'post-it', write the number of the rule that they should check and unobtrusively place it on students' papers.
5 As you correct compositions, you can also simply write the number of the rule when and where needed.

Box 54 A suggested list of rules for an intermediate class

- Put a period at the end of a sentence. Example: *Kumiko loves cats.*
- Start a new sentence with a capital letter. Example: *Her favorite cat is Bambo.*
- Put a question mark at the end of a sentence. Example: *Does Ahmed love American movies?*
- The first word after a question mark starts with a capital letter. Example: *Yes, Ahmed really loves American films – especially those with Kevin Costner.*
- A sentence must have a subject and a predicate and be a complete thought. Example: *Maria and Fabio went to a great party last week-end.*
- Put a comma before the word *and* in a compound sentence. Example: *We have studied English for six months, and we really feel that we have learned a lot.*
- Use *a* or *an* with singular count nouns when we are not really sure of who the person is. Example: *Herman arrived in a big car and a girl smiled at him. She gave him an apple.*
- Do not use *a* or *an* with a non-count noun. Example: *Sumi gave Theresa good advice.*
- Use *the* with nouns whose identity you know. Example: *The car that Herman arrived in was his father's.*

4.22 Letters of advice

Aim   writing, collaboration, fluency practice
Level   intermediate–advanced
Time   fluid

Procedure

1 In small groups, students are given a problem either as just a problem that needs a solution or a letter that asks for advice.
2 Students discuss the problem or the letter and either write a solution or write a letter that answers the advice seeker.
3 Students can write the letters in their own personae or you can add a role-play element by asking them to become teachers, psychologists, advice columnists, or social workers.
4 All groups can be working on the same letter or on the same problem, or you can give a different problem or letter to each group.
5 You could also give more advanced groups a series of problems and ask them to choose the one that seems most urgent.
6 After students have written the letters, each group reads its letter to the whole class and receives comments and suggestions.

See Boxes 55 and 56 for problems and letters posing problems.

Box 55 Good advice

- Give some good advice to a newly married couple.
- Give some good advice to the person who will rent your apartment next.
- Give some good advice to a first-time landlord.
- Give some good advice to a new student in your school or your institute.
- Give some good advice to a traveler who is going to visit a place you know well.

4.23 In the middle of the story

Aim   writing, fluency practice
Level intermediate–advanced
Time   fluid

Procedure

1 In small groups, students read the beginnings and endings of stories.
2 They discuss the possibilities of what happens in the middle.

Box 56 Letters with problems

Dear advisers,

Please help me out. I am getting married in July to Ken, a wonderful man. We have planned a perfect small wedding and are very happy, but here is the problem. We have arranged a wonderful honeymoon in England, a place that both Ken and I have always wanted to visit, and we were both so looking forward to it. Then suddenly Ken's parents decided that they wanted to join us. Now I really love Ken's parents and the last thing in the world that I want to do is to insult them, but honestly this is our honeymoon and I want to be alone with my husband. Ken says he doesn't care. He likes his parents and he says they won't bother us and he doesn't mind having them along, but I sure do! I am miserable about this. What should I do?

Unhappy bride

Dear advisers,

My daughter Kathy, who is fifteen years old, has always been messy. This has never really bothered me because I was very messy as a child too and I sort of grew out of it. I have let Kathy make as much of a mess as she wants to in her own room. I just never go in there, and once in a while, Kathy gets tired of the mess and cleans it up, so this has seemed like a good arrangement with me, but lately Kathy has been acting strangely, and I don't like the friends she brings home. My husband says we ought to go into Kathy's room when she isn't there and investigate what is going on. He is, of course, afraid of drugs. I feel that it is unethical to invade our daughter's privacy. What shall I do?

A confused mom

Dear advisers,

I have a job that I like very much, but there is no job security in it, and the pay is low. I love the town where I live and I have many good friends here. I also like my house and my neighborhood.

Now suddenly I have been offered a new job in a city far away where I don't know anyone. It is really a good job with much more pay, security, prestige, and possibility for promotion, but it is work that I am not really all that familiar with. I would have to learn many new things, and I don't know if I could become as good at it as the people who want to hire me evidently think that I can be. I would have to sell my house and buy one in the new city and start a whole new life. Is it really worth it? I have to add that even though I like my present job, I have been very frustrated because I feel that I just can't move on to anything better. Please tell me what to do.

Very troubled

3 Everyone contributes while a secretary writes the story.
4 A spokesperson from each group reads the story to the whole class. (See Box 57 for examples of beginnings and endings of stories.)
5 Volunteers from the class offer suggestions.

Note

You may wish to give all the groups the same story and hear interesting variations on a theme, or you may wish to give different stories to each group.

Box 57 Examples of beginnings and endings of stories

Story 1
Beginning
She stumbled and fell in a dark hole.

Ending
She was so glad to be home again.

Story 2
Beginning
He woke up with a crashing headache. Where was he? Nothing seemed familiar, and everything seemed gray. Somewhere there was a sound of water. 'So you are finally awake,' said a female voice to the left of him.

Ending
Lucy smiled. 'There never was anyone else in my life, Jack. It was always just you. Don't you know? I have loved you since I was twelve years old.'
And Jack knew that the world was just right again. Just the way it was supposed to be.

Story 3
Beginning
The lion was on top of him when he finally managed to pull the trigger, and then the dead beast was all over him, but he was alive and just had to dig his way out from under the enormous cat.

Ending
'Enough adventure,' Robert thought. 'I just want life to be very boring for a while.'

Story 4
Beginning
Once upon a time a beautiful princess was locked up in a high tower

---

by her father. The king was afraid that she would marry someone who wasn't just right, and so he kept her locked up until the day when he would find just the right man for her.

Ending
At the ball everyone had a good time and everyone was very happy – even the king.

Story 5
Beginning
It was too rainy to go out for a walk that Thursday, so I sat down in my favorite rocking chair and planned on reading the latest detective story that I had bought at the airport and not had time to read.

Ending
The beautiful ghost smiled. 'Oh, I will be back,' she said. 'I only hope that the next time you will not be so afraid of me.'

Story 6
Beginning
'Excuse me,' said the little white dog to Lucy. 'I am lost. Could you please help me find my people?'
Lucy was waiting in front of the ice-cream store, where her older sister Meg had just walked in to buy two ice-cream cones with the money Uncle David had given them.
'I didn't know that dogs could talk,' Lucy said.
'Well, please don't tell anyone' said the dog. 'It makes people very nervous. My name is Charles. What's yours?'

Ending
'He was my best friend,' Lucy said. 'But I am glad that he has found his people. They must have missed him very much.'

4.24 The spelling list

Aim   spelling, pair work
Level all levels
Time   fluid

Procedure

1 Ask students to analyze their own writing and discover the words that are difficult for them or that they frequently misspell.
2 Every so often, students give their list to a partner.

3 The partner tries to give some good ways of remembering the spelling. (See Box 58 for suggestions.)
4 Partners study their own lists.
5 Partners give each other a spelling test and mark it.
6 Words are reviewed.

Note

Many teachers have found it helpful to keep their own cumulative lists of frequently misspelled words and to use these for occasional reviews.

Box 58 Suggestions on remembering the spelling of words

Remember that in the word *meet* the two *ee*'s have a *meeting*.
Remember that in the word *meat* you *eat*.
Remember that in the word *week* e follows e just like day follows day in a week.
Remember that in the word *committee*, there are many twins sitting on the *committee* – two *ee*'s, two *t*'s and two *m*'s.
Remember that in the word *hear* there is an *ear*.

4.25 From words to story

Aim   writing, fluency practice, grammar review, gathering ideas
Level all levels
Time fluid

Procedure

1 Choose any subject, perhaps one that you have been reading about.
2 Divide the class into groups.
3 Assign different parts of speech to each group. Example: some groups think of all the nouns connected to the subject; other groups think of all the verbs connected to the subject; some brainstorm for adjectives.
4 Three secretaries come to the board. One will write up adjectives, one nouns and one verbs.
5 Volunteers from groups call out their words and the secretaries write them. As words are called out, students cross them off from their lists.

6 When all the lists have been made, groups write stories using as many words from the board as possible.
7 Group stories are read out to the whole class.

4.26 Plot construction

Aim writing, fluency practice
Level intermediate–advanced
Time fluid

Procedure

1 Divide the class into groups of five or six students each.
2 Assign different tasks to different groups. The tasks are: character; setting; problem; and solution. (See Box 59 for task descriptions.)
3 Groups brainstorm on the tasks.
4 Four secretaries go to the board and stand next to the four group headings.
5 Volunteers from the groups contribute suggestions, as the secretaries write them on the board.
6 In groups, students construct stories based on the information collected on the board.
7 The stories are read to the whole class.

Box 59 Task descriptions

Character: Give your person a name, an age, and an occupation. Describe his/her physical appearance.

Setting: Name and describe the place where the story will happen. Describe the climate of the location and how the place looks.
Example: *A small back street in the middle of downtown San Francisco. The houses are close together and are each painted a different color. There are small gardens and children play in the street. The weather is mostly warm.*

Problem: Give a specific problem like *a bad marriage* or *someone loses a lot of money* or *a traffic accident.*

Solution: Consider solutions for many kinds of problems.
Examples: *winning the lottery; a cure for a disease; meeting new people; finding a better job; getting an important gift.*

---

5 Working well in groups

The group as a natural framework for learning

The group seems to be a natural framework for the way ideas are worked with in the real world. People, on the whole, enjoy sharing ideas, learning from one another, and cooperating. In the workplace, people have discovered that cooperation is a much better tool than competition. Committees, boards, cohorts, and teams do the work of the world through communication. It seems only natural that the language classroom, which really is a laboratory in communication, should do a great deal of its work in groups.

In large multilevel classes, group work is obviously a key element as it enables students to learn from one another. When working in small groups, students have a greater chance to practice oral fluency. Students are also far less intimidated in a small group, and once they become familiar with the procedure, they usually enjoy sharing ideas and practicing new language structures in this format.

Some difficulties

Group work, however, does not always come easily to the classroom. Many classes are simply not used to working in groups and many even express a preference for the familiar teacher-fronted process. Another problem is that although the group is a place for growth and practice, it can also easily become a hidey-hole for the student who somehow assumes that the group's progress is automatically his/her own progress. It may therefore take some patience, consistent effort, and careful training to form effective group work.

Training for group work

Students need to learn how to work in group settings. They need to recognize the right of everyone to speak. They need to learn not to monopolize the group, and how to encourage the reticent and shy ones to speak. They need to practice specific group tasks, and to listen carefully to classmates. They need to learn how to present the group's efforts to the entire class and how to contribute to the collective group accomplishment. Activities 5.1, 5.2, and 5.8 are helpful in the development of a useful group process.

Creating an interesting balance

Group work is best used when it is not the only classroom interaction pattern, but when it is combined with many other strategies. Indeed, the large multilevel class works better when we provide a great deal of variety. We can plan our lessons to include teacher-fronted work, individual work, and pair work, as well as group work. If we plan correctly, our lessons will become an interesting balance between controlled practice in pairs, free practice in groups and individual performance through mingling strategies.

What usually works best

From long practice with group work, individual work and pair work, I have drawn certain conclusions:
1 Dialogue practice, vocabulary drill, and grammar review tend to work best as pair work.
2 Problem solving usually works best in groups of five.
3 Discussions seem to work best in triads.
4 Introductions and social interactions as a rule work best in groups of four and in mingling activities.

What happens if ... What happens when ... ?

During my work with teachers, certain questions about group work invariably come up. Those listed below, with my answers, are the ones most frequently asked.

Q: What happens if I feel that I have completely lost control of the class as they chat away in their groups?
A: This is a feeling many teachers experience when they first begin working with groups. Careful training of group procedure will eliminate much of this fear. Remember that even in the teacher-fronted classroom, you never really had complete control. There were always students daydreaming, passing notes, and doing their own thing. Language learning is a fairly chaotic activity, and language chaos can become very productive. Go with the flow for

a while. Some of the organizational activities below will help you to maintain a feeling of control and smooth process.

Q: What about the students who just sit in a group and never contribute?

A: This is most likely the student who would not contribute much in any framework, and chances are that the group structure will create some peer pressure that will motivate this student more than a teacher possibly could. Here are some possibilities to activate those passive students:

- Give them the task of group facilitator. (The person who has to see to it that everyone in the group gets a chance to speak.)
- Give them the task of 'encourager'. (The person who has to find something good in what other students say and point this out.)
- Let them be the ones that look up new words in the dictionary.
- Make a rule that during any group discussion, each group member must contribute to the discussion a certain number of times.
- Ask these students to be responsible for presenting the group summary.
- At the end of certain group activities ask all the students in the group to rate one another on participation and cooperation.

The activities in this chapter will provide you with more ideas. See especially activities 5.3, 5.4, and 5.9.

Q: What if students revert to the native language in their groups?

A: This is usually not a problem in multi-lingual classes where the target language is the only common language of the group. However, it can become a problem in the mono-lingual language class. I feel that an occasional lapse into the native language is not very harmful. The teacher who circulates among the groups can usually help by translating into the target language, and by simply being there to remind the group to stick to the target language. Also, you will notice that the task of group monitor, described in the activities below, helps keeping everyone on target. The important element here, which we will talk about much more in Chapters seven and eight, is to keep students responsible for their own learning and remove yourself from the policing and the law-enforcing role.

Q: What happens when some groups finish a task long before other groups?

A: It is always wise to have an extra activity for such groups. Consider letting them go over difficult vocabulary in the text, or perhaps create some good questions, or re-arrange the text differently, or discover interesting sentences. One of the simplest techniques is to give a basic minimal task that everyone can do with further extras that they can add on if/when they finish. For example, if you have assigned eight questions to be answered by each group, tell them to do a minimum of four. Or if the task is to place twelve words in certain places, ask the groups to do at least five. Such minimizing and maximizing creates a challenge for those who wish to forge ahead and allows the slower students to feel that they have accomplished what was expected.

This chapter has been divided into *organizational activities* that tell about how to best arrange the group process, and *content based activities* that describe how language works through the group process. You might have noticed that group activities are scattered throughout the book. This happens because group work does seem to be such a natural medium for the large heterogeneous class.

Organizational activities

5.1 Working together

Aim	cooperation, fluency practice, establishing rules
Level	all levels
Time	45–50 minutes
Preparation	Write on the board:

- The facilitator makes sure that everyone participates.
- The secretary summarizes what the group has talked about.
- The monitor keeps everyone on task speaking in the target language.
- The language provider looks words up in the dictionary or asks the teacher for help.

Procedure

1 Divide the class into groups of five.
2 For each group appoint an observer, who will stand.
3 Explain that, during part of every lesson, the class will be working in groups. After each group activity, all group members will sign their names on the group summary, and you will collect it.

4 Explain the function of each of the tasks that you have written on the board.
5 Give the groups a few minutes to decide who will function in each role. (One person in each group will not have a specific task.)
6 Stress that three things are important in group work:
  • participation
  • listening
  • learning from one another
7 Assign the group a task. (See Box 60 for examples.)
8 Explain that the job of the observer will be to note how well the three aims listed above are accomplished, and how well students function in their assigned roles.
9 Follow through with the task.
10 Monitors collect papers with students' signatures.
11 Monitors report to the whole class.
12 Repeat the procedure with another task. Make sure that group members assume new roles.

Notes

– Follow through on this procedure several times until you see that the class is functioning smoothly in groups.
– There is no need for you to read the group summaries very carefully. Just glance at them. The summary itself with students' signatures is the sign of commitment necessary for the process to flow smoothly.

Box 60 Possible group work tasks

• Sorting peanuts by size and/or shape.
• Deciding on how many number combinations make 36 (or any other number).
• Arranging loose sentence strips into a story.
• Arranging several pictures into story form and writing the story.
• Doing a crossword puzzle or a word-search.
• Writing a letter of complaint.
• Arranging a list of activities from most to least liked.
• Compiling a list of compliments for other members of the class.

5.2 The quiet signal

    Aim   organization, listening to directions, fluency practice

Level	all levels
Time	10–15 minutes

Preparation Decide on what your quiet signal (the signal for students to stop the group task and wait quietly) will be. (See Box 62 for suggestions.)

Procedure

1 Tell students that since language demands a lot of practice, much time in class will be spent on talking in pairs and in small groups. To do this successfully it is ***very important*** that everyone knows just when an activity starts, what everyone is supposed to do, and when an activity ends. This is why you will establish and stick with a certain quiet signal that everyone must know and recognize.
2 Show the class the quiet signal and tell them that you will spend some time practicing it.
3 Assign students a topic to talk about in pairs. (See Box 61 for suggestions.)
4 In pairs, students talk until the conversation seems animated and lively.
5 Use the quiet signal and time how long it takes the class to get quiet.
6 Say, 'Congratulations students. That only took you … minutes. But since we will have to do this many times during each lesson, I want it to go even faster. Let's see if we can practice one more time, and make the quiet signal work very, very quickly.'
7 Repeat the procedure with another topic.
8 Again, congratulate students, and if you feel that it is necessary repeat one more time.

Box 61 Suggestions for pair talk

- My favorite vacation
- A holiday I love
- A film I enjoyed
- My favorite restaurant
- What I like to do on weekends
- Wedding ceremonies
- Funeral ceremonies

Box 62 Suggestions for quiet signals

- Blinking over-head lights
- Ringing a bell
- Whistling with a whistle
- Ringing a tambourine
- Beating a drum
- Raising both arms upward – as soon as any students sees you do this, they should stop talking and follow suit until all arms are raised and quiet reigns.

Note

Use the quiet signal consistently, and it will serve you well! You will soon notice that students help you to implement it.

5.3   Give me your sticks

Aim	discussion, fluency practice, more even participation
Level	all levels
Time:	fluid
Preparation	Bring toothpicks to class – at least as many as five times the members of your class.

Procedure

1 Prior to any small group discussion, give each student five toothpicks.
2 Each time students speak up in the discussion, they place a toothpick in the center.
3 During the discussion, all toothpicks should be used.
4 Once all toothpicks are used, students are not allowed to talk unless they get special permission from the facilitator.
5 When the group discussion is over, ask 'How many of you used all five toothpicks?'. Get a show of hands and say, 'Great!'. Then ask, 'How many used four toothpicks?'. Again, get a show of hands and dole out praise. Continue with three, and say 'Good! Let's all try for five next time'.

Note

This activity ensures that over-participators don't steal the show during group discussion and it encourages those who are shy to speak up. Using this technique frequently promotes even participation.

Content based activities

5.4 The text jigsaw

Aim   reading, summarizing, writing, explaining, fluency practice

Level   all levels

Time   45–55 minutes

Preparation Divide any text you want to study into four sections and copy enough of each section of the text for a quarter of your class. Label the sections A, B, C, and D. Go through all the A's and number them all 1–4. Do the same for B's, C's, and D's. Prepare some comprehension and interpretation questions on the reading.

Procedure

1 Put the A, B, C, and D sections in stacks on your desk.
2 Students say *A, B, C, D* in turn around the class, thus assigning themselves these letters.

3 Check to see if everyone knows which letter is theirs by saying, *Will everyone who has letter A raise their hand.* Continue with all letters.
4 Point out to students that there is also a number on their papers and that they will later need these numbers.
5 Students pick up their letter reading from your desk.
6 Students read their individual reading silently. Circulate to help out with vocabulary.
7 **Peer groups.** In small groups, students meet those who have read the same **letter** reading.
8 In these small groups, students clarify the reading to one another and summarize it. Each person in the group should have a brief written summary.
9 **Expert groups.** In groups of four, students meet classmates who have the same **number** on their paper. These will be groups in which everyone has read a different section.
10 In the **Expert groups,** starting with A and followed by B, C, D, students tell one another about their readings. (Don't worry if there is more than one letter representative in a group. They will just help each other.)
11 In the **Expert groups,** students re-read their individual sections, choosing one sentence that seems particularly important or meaningful to them. They underline this sentence.
12 In the **Expert groups,** students read out their sentences and explain why they have chosen their sentences.
13 Students return to peer groups.
14 In the **Peer groups,** students once more read out and explain the sentences they have underlined.
15 As a whole class, discuss the reading by asking comprehension and interpretation questions.

Optional follow-up

If you can make enough copies of the entire reading for the whole class, you could assign the entire reading for homework and have a quiz on it the next day. This is a particularly useful technique for longer and more difficult readings.

Notes

– The preparations for the jigsaw may at first seem cumbersome, but the process is really very simple, and once you have gotten used to it, you will establish it as a routine that you use over and over again. The rewards of the jigsaw are enormous, as the technique uses all language skills and works very well across all levels and with any kind of content.

- If copying texts is a problem, use any longer text in the classbook you are using for jigsaw reading.
- The jigsaw works wonderfully in heterogeneous classes because even weaker students become experts.
- In some classes, you may wish to pre-teach some vocabulary before you begin the jigsaw.

Acknowledgement

I first read about the jigsaw in a book by Eliot Aaronson called *The Jigsaw Classroom*.

5.5 The picture jigsaw

Aim	fluency practice, vocabulary reinforcement, listening, writing
Level	intermediate–advanced
Time	20–30 minutes
Preparation	Have as many interesting pictures as you will have small groups in your class. They may be the kind of pictures that make a story or any kind of pictures. Try to include some pictures of people.

Procedure

1 Divide your class into small groups.
2 Each group gets a picture.
3 The group studies the picture and students decide how to best describe it.
4 Students put down the picture and describe it without looking at it.
5 Students look at the picture again to see if they have forgotten anything.
6 Collect the pictures.
7 Students meet in new small groups. In each small group there should be a representative of each picture.
8 Students tell one another about their pictures.
9 While all students in the groups contribute, a secretary writes the story they create around the pictures.
10 Place all the pictures in a visible place.
11 A representative from each group reads the group's story, while you re-arrange the pictures as they appear in the story if they make one.

Note

This activity becomes interesting because the stories are invariably all different.

5.6   Making mine long

Aim   writing, fluency practice, vocabulary expansion, listening

Level   intermediate–advanced

Time   45 minutes

Preparation   Write some very simple sentences that can easily be expanded. (See Box 63 for suggestions.) Have one sentence for each small group.

Procedure

1 With the whole class, demonstrate sentence expansion. For example: 'Write the sentence *The cat likes milk* on the board and ask the class to contribute words that would make the sentence more interesting. Students should contribute one word at a time as you or a secretary insert these words into the sentence. You could finish with a sentence that reads:
The big, gray, clever cat that belongs to my wonderful, eighty-two-year-old grandmother, who lives on eighty-second street in New York City on the 5th floor in a large apartment house, really and truly likes only chocolate flavored, slightly heated, evaporated milk in the afternoon.
2 Each small group gets a sentence and expands on it.
3 Each group reads out its sentence to the whole class.
4 A secretary from each group writes the group sentence on the board.
5 The class votes for the most original sentence. (Students are not allowed to vote for their own group.)

Box 63 Suggestions for simple sentences that can be used for sentence expansion

For intermediate/advanced students

- The young man was grateful to his aunt.
- My sister gave me a book.
- Father never understood his father.
- The man gave the woman a present.
- The man met his wife at the zoo.
- She enjoys movies.

For beginner students

- He loves to eat.
- The girl loved a boy.
- My mother cooks.
- I can read.
- I eat cake.
- Pizza is good.
- He can write.

5.7 Sentences into story

Aim   writing, fluency practice, vocabulary expansion, listening
Level   intermediate–advanced
Time   45 minutes

Procedure

1 In small groups, students each memorize a sentence from the suggested sentences in Box 63 or from sentences you have written up on the board for them.
2 Students check to see that each group member has a different sentence.
3 Students combine the sentences into a story, adding words and phrases when needed.
4 A spokesperson from each group reads the group's story to the whole class.

Optional follow-ups

- Collect all the stories and make enough copies for the whole class. Let the class vote for its favorite story. (They are not allowed to vote for their own.)
- Assign groups that did not write the story to peer edit it.
- Let groups that did not write stories expand and change another group's story and have the new versions read in class.

5.8   The aquarium

Aim   discussion, fluency practice, listening

Level   intermediate–advanced

Time   fluid

Preparation   Have a list of interesting discussion topics. Each topic should be accompanied by a lead-in question. (See Box 64 for suggestions.)

Procedure

1 Divide your class into small groups.
2 Group joins group.
3 One of the two groups takes seats for comfortable discussion, while the second group forms a standing circle around the first group. The sitting group is the **aquarium**.
4 The aquarium group begins the discussion of the topic.
5 Anyone from the outside observer group who wants to join the discussion taps a member of the aquarium on the shoulder and the two exchange places.
6 Circulate among the groups and occasionally join an aquarium by tapping someone on the shoulder.
7 Let the discussions go as long as there seems to be interest.
8 If you notice that one group is unenthusiastic while another seems to be going full steam, ask the less enthusiastic group to join the flourishing one.
9 In some classes, there may finally be just one aquarium going while the rest are observers who keep floating in and out of the aquarium.

Box 64 Discussion topics with opening questions

- Peace in the world is impossible. Why have there always been wars?
- Teenagers should not be going to school. They should work. Why is there so much violence in schools today?
- Owning guns should be illegal. Why are so many people killed with guns?
- Women can do anything that men do in the world of work. Should women be generals?
- We must stop eating animals. Do we have the right to eat animals?
- Machines will eventually take over the world. Are people like machines?
- There are far too many road accidents. Should we have stricter driving laws?
- There is still hunger in the world. What can we do to make sure that nobody in the world starves?
- Many people die because they don't get proper medical treatment. What must we do to give every child born a chance for good health?
- Many people in the world today are illiterate. How can we teach the world to read?

5.9 All for one

Aim	fluency practice, group cooperation, review
Level	all levels
Time	fluid

Preparation Prepare a set of questions on any material you have studied. These can be comprehension questions, fill the blank questions, true and false questions or any other format you wish to use.

Procedure

1 Students sit in groups of five.
2 In each group count off from one to five, and each student is assigned a number between one and five.

3 To check that the above has been accomplished, say, 'Will all the ones raise their hands'. Continue with all five numbers.
4 Assign a letter name to each group – A, B, C, D according to how many groups are in your class.
5 Ask your first question.
6 Allow students one minute to work together in their group to get the answer. They should make sure that everyone in the group knows the answer.
7 Call out a random number between one and five.
8 The students whose number has been called stand.
9 Ask the student in group A for the answer. (At this time, he/she is not allowed help from the group.) If this student knows, his/her group earns a point. If he/she doesn't know, the question moves to the next group.
10 Keep this going until you have finished all your questions, and announce the group winner.

5.10 Group dictations

Aim	writing, clear speech, listening, dictation practice, review or preview
Level	all levels
Time	15–20 minutes
Preparation	Find a suitable passage to be dictated. It may be a passage from a text you have recently studied, and thus it will serve as a review, or it may be a passage from a text that you will soon read, and thus will serve as preview. The passage should not be longer than about half a page of text.

Procedure

1 Divide the class into groups of five.
2 Each group sends a reader to the front of the room.
3 Give each reader the passage to be dictated.
4 Groups send another student who meets the group reader.
5 The reader reads the first sentence to the group emissary. The emissaries may ask for as many repetitions as they need. They can also ask for only half of the sentence. (**But the reader is not allowed to show the text to the emissary.**)
6 The emissary returns to the group and dictates what he heard while group members write. They may ask for repetitions, and the emissaries can go back and ask the reader for repetitions as many times as they wish.
7 When you notice fatigue on the part of the emissaries, call *Switch*. This will be a signal for groups to send new emissaries. The former emissaries will join the groups and continue the dictation of the previous writers.
8 Do several switches.
9 When one group is finished with the entire passage, declare that group the winner.
10 Give each group the entire passage and allow some time for them to check their work.
11 Ask for a correct reading of the entire passage.

5.11 The community group project

Aim   group participation, extensive reading, research, getting to know the community, fluency practice

Level advanced

Time   fluid

Procedure

1 Suggest aspects of the community for students to investigate. (See Box 65 for suggestions.)
2 Show your list to the class and ask for further suggestions. Set a date for when the presentations have to be completed and given. Give a period of about two weeks for preparation.
3 Divide the class into groups of six. Two group members will find readings that deal with the subject and make enough copies for all six members. Two group members will interview people in the

community connected to the subject, and report their findings to the group. Two members of the group will organize the presentation, and assign presentation tasks to all group members. The presentation should be accompanied by some visual aid such as an overhead projector, a video, a poster, or a picture.

4 Groups meet and decide on their topic, and who is to do what. They appoint a chairperson who is to be in charge of the whole project. They exchange telephone numbers and decide when their first outside-of-class meeting will be held.

5 On presentation day, students organize and set up visual aids before class. In class, they make ten to fifteen minute presentations. The chairperson introduces all speakers and states the goals of the project. Each student should do some aspect of the group's presentation.

6 At the conclusion of the presentations, everyone present fills out the evaluation form. (See Box 66 for an example of an evaluation form.)

Notes

– This activity works best in the ESL framework. However, I have used it in the EFL setting by sending students to those community aspects that dealt with tourism – hotels, museums, fundraising institutions.

– Inviting guests or another class makes presentation day more special.

– People from the community who have been interviewed are usually happy to come.

– This activity works well as a culminating project for an advanced class.

– The comments and suggestions on the evaluation forms will be useful to you when you plan your next project presentation.

Box 65 Suggestions for projects

- An interesting museum
- A hospital
- A library
- A park
- A zoo
- City planning
- A farming community
- Transportation in the community
- Theater arts in the community
- Higher education

Box 66 Example of evaluation form

Student's name ....

Name of presentation ....

By doing the presentation I learned ....

....

....

Our presentation would have been better if ....

....

I think that doing this project was useful/not useful because

....

....

From the presentations by other students that I observed, I liked

....

best because ....

....

5.12 The walk-about

Aim	reading, speaking, listening, text review, homework check
Level	all levels
Time	20–30 minutes
Preparation	Cut a set of assigned questions into strips and tape the strips in various places along the walls of the classroom. Also, have a set of these questions ready for each student.

Procedure

1 In pairs, students walk around the classroom from question to question. One student stands with his back to the wall, while his/her partner reads the question. The listening student answers the question. If he/she doesn't know the answer, the pair can work on it together, or they can turn to another pair or to the teacher for help.
2 In the next question, the student who previously read becomes the listener.
3 Students move around the room until they have answered all the questions or you have stopped them.
4 Distribute a copy of the entire set of questions to all students.
5 In small groups, students work on the entire set of questions.
6 In plenary, talk about some of the most interesting or puzzling questions.

5.13 Picture puzzle

Aim	fluency practice, listening, writing
Level	intermediate–advanced
Time	30–40 minutes
Preparation	Get one picture for every four students. Cut each picture into four pieces. Put each set of four pieces in an envelope. Bring tape.

Procedure

1 Give each group of four an envelope.
2 In groups of four, each student pulls a quarter of a picture from the envelope without letting those in their group see what is in the picture.
3 Each teammate describes his/her part of the picture without showing it.
4 Without looking at the whole picture, the group decides what the picture probably looks like.
5 They put their pieces together and see how correct their verbal description was.

Optional follow-up

− Two groups meet and put the two pictures together into a story. A secretary writes up the story.
− Representatives from each group of eight present the story and show the pictures to the entire class.

5.14 Back and forth movie preview/in view

Aim	fluency practice, film preview
Level	intermediate–advanced
Time	15–20 minutes
Preparation	Get an interesting film and have a VCR and TV ready.

Procedure

1 In pairs, one student stands so that he/she can see the TV screen, while another student sits with his/her back to the TV set.
2 Show the first scene of the film with the sound off.
3 The standing student tells his/her partner what is going on in the film.
4 After a few minutes call *Switch*, and the partners switch sitting and standing positions.
5 Continue this telling and switching until the end of the first scene.
6 In small groups, students summarize what they have seen, what they assume that this was all about, and what will happen later in the film.
7 In plenary, groups report.
8 Play the scene with the sound on.
9 In small groups, students talk about how the sound made a difference.
10 In plenary, groups report.
11 Continue showing the film. Periodically stop to allow students to predict what will happen next.
12 Periodically stop the film to do steps one to seven with any interesting scene in the film.

5.15 Three in one

Aim	reading, speaking, review or preview
Level	beginners–intermediate
Time	10–20 minutes
Preparation	Choose sentences from a reading you have recently done with your class or one that you plan to do. Choose enough sentences for one third of your class. Write

the sentences on strips of paper and cut each strip into three pieces, so that there is a third of the sentence on each piece of strip.

Procedure

1 Each student gets a piece of strip.
2 Students mingle, reading out their strip to classmates until they find the other two students that form a sentence with them.
3 In groups of three, students read their sentence.
4 Each group reads out its sentence to the entire class.
5 Students look at the passage from which the sentences were taken and locate their own sentence.
6 In their groups, students read the sentence that preceded their own and the one that followed it.

5.16 The missing word

Aim	vocabulary study
Level	beginners–intermediate
Time	20–30 minutes
Preparation	Choose eight to ten words that you want to review. Write each word on a large index card.

Procedure

1 In small groups, students review the meaning and spelling of the words.
2 Each group gives itself a name.
3 Write the names across the board.
4 Line up the index cards in a visible place in the front of the class.
5 Appoint a scorekeeper.
6 Each small group sends a representative to the front.
7 The group representatives study the card lineup.
8 They turn their backs to the cards.
9 Remove one card and re-arrange the card order.
10 The students in front turn to look at the cards.
11 The first student to shout out the missing word scores a point for his group.
12 New group representatives come to the front, and the procedure is repeated as long as interest is high.

5.17 Alphabet shopping

Aim   vocabulary expansion
Level   beginners–intermediate
Time   20–30 minutes

Procedure

1 Review all the words you have studied that have to do with foods. Let the class contribute words they might have picked up in places other than class. Allow time for looking in the dictionary. Put all new words on the board. Allow some time for study, then erase.
2 In small groups, students go through the alphabet, trying to contribute as many food items as possible for each letter.
3 Stop the activity when you notice that most groups have done about all they can.
4 The first group gives all its contributions under A. When an item is mentioned, it is crossed off everyone's list.
5 The next group gives the B's. Continue throughout the alphabet. The group that has items no one has mentioned is the winner.

Variation

You can, of course, do the same activity with a variety of vocabulary categories like, for example, furniture, clothes, or animals.

5.18 Pronoun search

Aim   grammar review, scanning a text
Level   beginners–intermediate
Time   fluid
Preparation   Choose a text that has a variety of pronouns in it, preferably a text that you have already studied with your students.

Procedure

1 Explain that a pronoun is a word that takes the place of a noun. Examples: *I, you, he, she, it, we, you, they, who, whom.*

2 In small groups, students find as many pronouns and antecedents (the word that the pronoun refers to) as they can in the text.
3 The first group reads out the pronouns and antecedents they found in the first sentence of the text. As soon as a pronoun is mentioned, it is crossed off everyone's list.
4 The second group does the same with the next sentence. Continue until the text has been covered. The group that has a pronoun that no one has found is the winner.

Variation

You can, of course, do the same activity with a variety of grammatical categories like, for example, verbs, adjectives, or nouns.

5.19 Words to make a cake

>**Aim** vocabulary expansion, writing, speaking
>**Level** beginners–intermediate
>**Time** fluid

Procedure

1 Together with the whole class, elicit all the words needed to make a cake (*flour, sugar, milk, butter, cocoa, raisins, eggs*). Write these words on the board as they come up.
2 Review all the verbs needed to describe cake making (*mix, stir, add, pour, break*). Write these words on the board as they come up.
3 In small groups, students review the words.
4 When you are reasonably sure that everyone knows the words, erase them from the board.
5 In small groups, students write a recipe for a special cake.
6 A representative from each group reads the recipe of the group.

Optional follow-up

In some classes students have actually gone home and baked the cakes which they brought in the next day to share with the class.

Variation

You can, of course, vary this exercise to other products like, for example, building a house, making a dress, or cooking a stew.

5.20 Things we share

Aim   fluency practice, group cohesion

Level beginners–intermediate

Time   10–15 minutes

Procedure

1 In groups of three, students talk about their families, the things they like to do, and/or the foods they like to eat.
2 The goal is to find at least two things that they all have in common.
3 Stop the discussion after an agreed upon time, and ask the groups to report to the whole class.

5.21 Our group cheer

Aim   vocabulary expansion, group cohesion

Level beginners–intermediate

Time   10–15 minutes

Procedure

1 Ask each group to give itself a name.
2 Explain the meaning of 'a cheer' (words that you shout to cheer someone).
3 Together with the class, elicit good words that describe people. Examples: *smart, beautiful, brave, energetic, interesting, incredible, great, terrific.*
4 Each group picks two adjectives that describe them. They create a cheer, which consists of the first adjective repeated three times and ending with the second adjective and their group name. Example: *Smart! Smart! Smart! Terrific! The Tigers!*
5 Each group shouts its cheer.

5.22 **Dictated stories**

Aim	reading, writing, speaking, grammar review, vocabulary review
Level	all levels
Time	fluid

Procedure

1 Dictate key words from a passage you have recently studied.
2 In small groups, students reconstruct the passage.
3 Each group dictates a sentence from its reconstructed passage as you write it on the board.
4 Ask students to help you correct the grammar as you write.
5 When the passage is on the board, the class reads it chorally.
6 Frame certain words in the passage and ask individual students to read and explain these words.

5.23 **Three good questions**

Aim	predicting
Level	intermediate–advanced
Time	fluid

Procedure

1 Before you read about the topic, give them the central idea or title and ask them to construct three good questions about the topic.
2 In small groups, students construct the questions.
3 Write the questions up on the board as students volunteer them.
4 Volunteers answer some or all of the questions.
5 As you proceed with your reading, refer back to the questions.

6 Individualizing and personalizing student work

In large classes, it is important to create activities that will keep the more advanced students interested and at the same time allow the less advanced students to make progress at their own pace. How do we accomplish this? Sometimes students accomplish the task for us by finding their own level in language progression, and this very much depends on the level of their motivation. All of us have had students who conquered material which we thought was way beyond their present level. I have a very fond memory of a beginning student, Maria Lopez, who insisted, against all advice, on joining my advanced ESL class. The class was reading *My Antonya* by Willa Cather. Maria must have looked up every word in her bilingual dictionary. Then she went home and wrote her book review in Spanish. An advanced student helped her to translate the review into perfect English. She memorized the review and was able to write it in class. Within six months Maria had learned enough English to enroll in a college course and, five years later, she had a Master's degree and was speaking and writing English like a native speaker with only a bare trace of a charming Latino accent on her speech. Maria is not the only one who has decided on where she stands in her language progress and how far and how fast she is willing and able to go. Many students do this, even if not on such a dramatic scale as Maria's, and in much of our teaching, we can assume that students will drift toward their own level of progress.

However, as we all know, most of our students are not like Maria, but do need to be supplied with challenges that are nearer to their level. This is where multilevel activities are useful and create a more pleasant and accessible climate in our classrooms.

There are basically two ways of modifying activities to make them multilevel - individualization and personalization. When we individualize a task, we allow students to approach it on several different levels. When we personalize a task, we allow students to make it very much their own by giving them opportunities to express their own individual opinions, experiences and feelings as well as working on it on a level appropriate to them.

Individualizing

You can individualize task in two ways – you can use the same material in different ways, or you can use different materials in the same way. You can, for example, take one text, and ask some students to answer difficult inference questions on it, while other students answer simple factual questions. That would be an example of using the same material in different ways. You could also choose two texts on a common theme, making one an unabridged text and the second an abridged text. Later you could give students a set of questions which related to both texts. In pairs made up of a student who read the unabridged text and one who read the abridged text, students would be able to help each other. That would be an example of using different material in the same way. In this chapter, you will find more examples of such strategies.

6.1   Multilevel dictation

Aim	listening, writing, spelling, multilevel progress
Level	all levels
Time	20–30 minutes

Preparation   Choose a passage for dictation. Students will have studied the passage at home or in class. Create four different levels of the passage by:
  – using a blank page for the most advanced level.
  – leaving out great chunks of text on the next level.
  – leaving out smaller sections of text in the less difficult level.
  – leaving out only small sections in the least difficult level, which will look like a cloze passage.

Make enough copies of each level for your class. Arrange four stacks of papers – corresponding to the four levels – on your desk. For the purpose of checking, make enough copies of the original passage for your entire class.

Procedure

1 From the stacks on your desk, students choose a paper according to the level they think is best suited for them.
2 Dictate the passage, while students write and complete papers on their chosen level.
3 Re-read the passage, to allow students to check their work.
4 Hand out the original passage and allow students to check their

own work and to give themselves a score.

5 Students pass their papers to the front so that you can look them over to decide what the problematic areas are.

Notes

– Encourage your students to move to higher levels.
– In some circumstances, you might prefer to distribute the papers yourself making sure that students get papers at the appropriate level.

6.2 The book cart

Aim	individualized reading, writing reports, fluency practice
Level	mixed ability
Time	fluid
Preparation	On a movable cart collect books and magazines of all levels of difficulty. Prepare sign-out sheets in a loose-leaf notebook.

Procedure

1 Once a week on a designated day, bring in the cart to your classroom.
2 Allow students to browse and to check out books or magazines. Those who have already chosen material can read.
3 When all students have chosen their reading for the following week, ask those who think that they read something good that they would like to recommend to others to stand.
4 Students cluster around those who can recommend good reading, and listen to what they have to say.

Optional follow-up

Students hand in the reading review of the previous week. (See Box 67 for a sample of a reading review.)

Notes

– Appoint a student to be librarian and handle the sign-in and check-out process.
– Encourage students to contribute books and magazines to the cart.
– The reading reviews are deliberately very simple. This is meant to be a free reading activity and not necessarily a writing activity. I have found that often students don't read simply because they cannot bear the thought of writing a lengthy review.

Box 67 Sample of a reading review

Student's name: ....

Title of reading ....

Author ....

Number of pages ....

Did you enjoy the reading? Please explain why or why not.

....

....

Do you think that this reading helped to improve your English?
Please explain.

....

....

....

© Cambridge University Press 2001

6.3   Silent task work with a self-access box

Aim	varied skill practice
Level	mixed ability
Time	fluid

Preparation   In a box that you can move from class to class,
prepare a variety of material. You can keep adding to it at all
times. The material may include articles with tasks attached,
pictures that should be described, objects that can be described,
grammar exercises from books you no longer use, or any
other material that you deem appropriate. (See Box 68 for
suggestions.) Each project should, when possible, include an
answer sheet on which students can check their work. In a
pocket attached to the box, keep completion papers that the
students fill out when they are finished with a task.

Procedure

1 Distribute the first task to students to get them going.
2 As students finish it, they hand it in to you with a completion sheet. (See Box 69 for an example.)
3 As students complete the task, they go to the box to choose another.
4 As they finish each task, they fill out a completion sheet.

Variation

You can use the self-access box in other lessons. For example, if you have set individual or group work on a set activity or exercise and find that some students finish early, these students can simply get tasks from the self-access box.

Notes

– Encourage students to bring in more ideas for projects.
– More able students can be put to work writing project instructions.

Box 68 Suggested tasks for the self-access box

- Writing test questions on a recently read passage.
- Simplifying a text.
- Writing answers to a set of questions.
- Translating a passage into the native language. Then putting away the original and retranslating their own translation into English and checking this with the original.
- Writing a first or second draft of a composition.
- Journal writing.
- Grammar exercises.
- Outlining a reading passage.
- Doing a mind-map of a recently read article.
- Creating a crossword puzzle.
- Writing sentences with newly acquired vocabulary words.
- Correcting a dictation that has mistakes.
- Filling the blanks in a cloze passage.
- Reading an article and finding the main idea.
- Describing an object.

Box 69 Sample of task completion sheet

Student's name ....

My project today was ....

I chose to do this because ....

I enjoyed/did not enjoy doing this because ....

....

The part that I found most difficult was ....

....

The part that I thought was the easiest was ....

....

6.4 Working with words

Aim	mastering vocabulary
Level	mixed ability
Time	fluid

Preparation   Write a list of words that students have already been exposed to through a text that you have recently studied. Write the definitions in jumbled order on a different place on the board. Construct a set of sentences in which each word from the list has been left as a blank. For example, if one of my words were *clown*, I would write: *In the circus, a . . . makes people laugh.*

Procedure

1 Give students a choice of four tasks:
   - They can write sentences that include the words, preferably two of the words in each sentence.
   - They can match the word and its definition.
   - They can find the text through which they learned these words and copy the sentence where the words appeared.
   - They can listen to you or a student read the sentences where words fit into the blanks and write the sentences including the missing words.

2 Students who finish one task in the given time, can go on to another of the tasks.
3 With the whole class check all of the tasks. Make sure that you listen to several varieties of the original sentences.

6.5 Sentence completion

Aim	vocabulary review, writing
Level	mixed ability
Time	fluid
Preparation	Create ten sentence openings, each one to include a word that you want to recycle. For example, if the word I want to recycle is *rejected*, I might write: *He felt that his mother rejected him because . . .*

Procedure

1 Read out a sentence opening. Stop and allow students time to complete the sentence in writing.
2 Listen to several completed sentences read out loud.
3 Ask if everyone understands the word, and if it isn't quite clear ask for more examples and definitions.
4 Continue in this way with all the words.

Optional follow-up

Write some of the completions on the board.

Notes

– It is very important to stop and listen to the readings immediately after each sentence when the struggle of it is still in students' minds. The exercise will be less effective if you allow students to finish all ten sentences before you check.
– Make sure that you call on different people for the completions.

6.6 Question the reading

Aim	reading, fluency practice, sharing information, listening
Level	intermediate–advanced
Time	45 minutes

> **Preparation**   Choose a fairly short and interesting reading. Make out a set of comprehension questions on the reading. Make enough copies to give each B group one copy of the questions and each A group one reading for each student.

Procedure

1 Assign students to small groups and label the groups A or B. The B groups should consist of the stronger students.
2 Give the story to a reader in each of the B groups.
3 Give the question sheet to a reader in each of the A groups.
4 The A groups read the text twice. They take turns, reading a few lines each.
5 While the A groups are listening to the text being read, the B groups are writing down the questions which the reader dictates. They should pass the paper around in their group so that everyone gets a chance to be the reader.
6 Each student finds a partner from the other group.
7 The B students read out their questions and the A students answer them.
8 Repeat steps 6 and 7 with different partners.
9 Students pair up with new A and B combination partners. The A partners read the text to the B partners.
10 The B partners give the A partners the questions.
11 The A partners ask the questions and the B partners answer.

Personalizing

6.7   Vocabulary cards

Aim	keeping track of one's own words
Level	mixed ability
Time	fluid
Preparation	Bring a stack of index cards.

Procedure

1 Give several index cards to each student. They will be expected to provide their own from this point on.

2 Students write each new word on one side of the card.
3 On the second side they write anything that will be helpful for them to remember the word – it can be the translation, any mnemonic that helps them, and an original sentence with the word.
4 Sometimes during each lesson, students flip through the cards to see how well they remember the words.
5 In pairs students check each other on their words.
6 When students are sure that they know some words, they ask a partner to quiz them and if they truly know these words, the cards get thrown away.
7 Encourage students to keep their cards handy in a purse or pocket so that they can review them as they wait for a bus or stand in line at the supermarket or wait for a friend to show up for an appointment.

6.8 Three minute talks

Aim   fluency practice, confidence building, class cohesion
Level   mixed ability
Time   fluid
Preparation Prepare a large calendar that can be displayed somewhere in the class. Attach pencil and eraser to it.

Procedure

1 Hand out a list of topics for short speeches. (See Box 70 for suggestions.)
2 Students sign up on the calendar, three students each day. Encourage students to write down their date on their personal calendar. During a term students can make several three minute talks.
3 The speeches should not be longer than three minutes with the maximum of a one minute over-time.
4 Appoint a time keeper, who will warn speakers when their time is up, by holding up a card marked *three minutes up*.
5 Each talk can be followed by questions.
6 Encourage speakers to say *Are there any questions?*

Note

This activity works best if everyone takes the same topic and then everyone moves on to another topic. There are so many variations on one theme that the interest is always high.

Box 70 Suggestions for three minute speech topics

- A hope for the future
- A good decision in my life
- A dream I have always had
- A goal for the next five years
- A big change in my life
- Something I am afraid of
- Something I am proud of

Acknowledgement

I first learned about three minute speeches from my creative colleague Kevin Keating at the Center for English As a Second Language at the University of Arizona.

6.9 The story of my life posters

Aim	fluency practice, writing, class cohesion
Level	mixed ability
Time	fluid

Preparation Create a poster briefly telling the story of your life. Use pictures from magazines and make headings with markers. Put in whatever you consider appropriate. (See Box 71 for an example.) Bring markers, old magazines, glue and/or glue sticks, tape, large papers. Encourage your students to bring more. Ask colleagues to contribute old magazines.

Procedure

1 Show the class your poster and relate the story of your life.
2 Working together in groups, students help one another produce life story posters.
3 In small groups, students present their posters to one another.
4 Posters are put up on walls around the classroom.
5 Three to five students volunteer to be presenters of posters. The rest of the class walks from poster session to poster session listening to presentations.
6 Throughout the term, different students volunteer for a repeat of step 5.

on

d of putting the words in a house, ask students to place them in
neighborhood. Example: *I would put the word 'parenthesis' in the*
because parentheses look so much like trees.

onal follow-up

students to mentally wander through their house or neighborhood,
ing to remember where they have put each word.

cknowledgement

learned this activity in a workshop given by Mario Rinvolucri.

6.12 The mailbox

Aim	writing, individual expression, class cohesion
Level	mixed ability
Time	15–20 minutes
Preparation	Have a box or a bag ready to serve as the mailbox.

Procedure

1 Students write their names on slips of paper.
2 Collect the slips in a bag.
3 Each student pulls a slip with another student's name.
4 They write a letter to the person on the slip and deposit their letter
  in the mailbox. (See Box 73 for suggestions on topics to write
  about.)
5 In the following lesson, a student who serves as mailperson delivers
  the letters.
6 Students answer the letters, and deposit them in the mailbox.

Notes

– Encourage students to ask questions of their letter partners.
– If you collect the name slips and keep them in an envelope marked for
  the class, you will eliminate step one in future uses of the activity.
– This activity can be repeated many times as students get to know one
  another.

Box 71 Example of life poster

ANIKA'S LIFE STORY

ANIKA IS BORN

ANIKA GOES TO A GIRLS' SCHOOL IN STOCKHOLM

ANIKA GETS HER FIRST HORSE, FLIKA

ANIKA SPENDS MUCH TIME WITH FLIKA

ANIKA DECIDES TO BECOME A HORSEBREEDER

VET SCHOOL

ANIKA GOES TO AMERICA TO LEARN ENGLISH AND STUDY AT A FAMOUS VETERINARY SCHOOL

6.10 My object

Aim	fluency practice, class cohesion
Level	mixed ability
Time	15–20 minutes
Preparation	Bring some interesting object in with you to share with your class.

Procedure

1 From your handbag or your pocket pull an object. It needn't be anything terribly significant. (See Box 72 for suggestions.)
2 Tell the class what the object is and why you carry it with you. Example: *This is my pill box. I carry it with me because it reminds me to take my medicine. My sister gave it to me as a present and I really like it.*
3 In small groups, students talk about their objects.
4 Each group chooses one object to be talked about with the entire class.
5 A spokesperson from each group explains the group object – this should not be the owner of the object.
6 In plenary, hold up any of the group objects and ask *Who remembers anything about this object?*
7 Repeat step 6 with two other objects.
8 Repeat steps 3–8 as long as there is interest.

Box 72 Examples of objects

- Pens
- Diaries
- Keys
- Wallets
- Photo albums
- Calendars
- Good luck charms
- Pill boxes
- Notebooks
- Combs
- Make-up kits

6.11 The vocabulary house

Aim	vocabulary review, fluen
Level	mixed ability
Time	15–20 minutes
Preparation	On the board have a list of v to review.

Variati

Instea
their
park

Op
As
tr

Procedure

1 Students draw a floor plan of the house, apartment, o they now live.

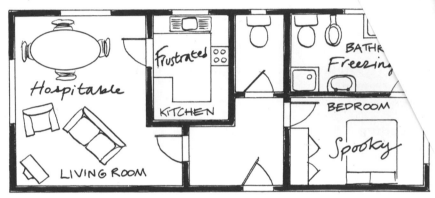

2 It is the job of the students to put as many words from the list into places in their house and to know and be able to explain why they have put each word in its particular place.
3 Give them an example by saying something like *Oh, here is the word 'frustrated'. I would put 'frustrated' in my kitchen because I hate to cook, and I always feel frustrated when I try.*
4 Students stand and mingle. They meet classmates and tell them where they placed one of their words and why they did it that way. Then they move on to another classmate and repeat the procedure.
5 Continue as long as interest is high.

Note

In most of my classes I ask students to draw a 'vocabulary house' on a very large piece of paper at the beginning of our session. They fold this paper and keep it in their class notebook and keep adding new words to it as we go along.

Box 73 Suggested topics for letters

- Something interesting that happened recently
- A current event
- My family
- A holiday I enjoy
- A good place to meet people
- A good place to practice English
- Music I love
- Something I used to do but I no longer do
- Something I wish we would do in this class
- A plan for the future
- Where I want to travel

6.13 My machine

Aim	fluency practice, individual expression, class cohesion
Level	mixed ability
Time	15–20 minutes

Procedure

1 In small groups, students brainstorm for a list of machines that are useful in their lives.
2 Get feedback from all groups and create a class list on the board.
3 Each student chooses a machine which is most like him/her. Example: *I am like a popcorn popper because I think quickly and have many ideas.*
4 Students stand and mingle. They meet classmates and talk about why they are like a certain machine.

Variation

Do the same with animals, instead of machines.

6.14 An important decision

Aim fluency practice, individual expression, class cohesion

Level mixed ability

Time 15–20 minutes

Procedure

1 Students write down three important decisions they have made in their lives.
2 Students choose one of these decisions to talk about.
3 Students stand and mingle, telling one another about their important decision and why it was important.
4 With the whole class, talk about why making an important decision can be so difficult.

Optional follow-up

Students write about their important decision.

Note

The activity is a good introduction to any reading that deals with decisions. Examples of such readings are: *The Road not Taken* by Robert Frost or *Eveline* by James Joyce.

6.15 An important sentence

Aim reading review, individual expression, fluency practice

Level mixed ability

Time 15–20 minutes

Procedure

1 After the class has read a passage together, ask students to read it again and underline one sentence or phrase that they consider most meaningful to them, or perhaps a sentence that they agree or disagree with.
2 In small groups, students read out their sentences and explain why they chose this particular sentence.
3 Volunteers from the groups tell the whole class about a phrase or sentence that they have chosen.

6.16 Color sadness blue

Aim vocabulary review, fluency practice, individual expression, class cohesion
Level intermediate–advanced
Time 15–20 minutes

Procedure

1 Use any list of words that the class has recently worked on. Put these words on the board.
2 Review all colors.
3 Students give each word a color. They should know why they are using this particular color. Example: *I colored the word 'exercise' green because I like to run outside when it is spring and everything is green.*
4 Students stand and mingle. They tell one another how and why they colored their words.
5 In plenary, volunteers tell the class about any unusual coloring that they encountered as they mingled.

6.17 Water words

Aim vocabulary review, individual expression, class cohesion
Level intermediate–advanced
Time 15–20 minutes

Procedure

1 In small groups, students brainstorm for words associated with water. Get them started by giving a few examples such as *shower, lake, tears.*
2 Get feedback from the groups and create a blackboard list.
3 Draw students' attention to particularly difficult vocabulary items you have recently taught.
4 Students associate each vocabulary item with a water word. Example: *The word 'compelled' goes with 'lake' because when I was little my brother compelled me to swim in a cold lake.*

5 Students stand and mingle. They share their associations with class-mates.
6 In plenary, volunteers tell the class about interesting associations that they heard from classmates.

Variation

You can do the same activity using jewelry instead of water.

6.18 I don't like people who

> **Aim** fluency practice, practice with the relative pronoun *who*, individual expression, class cohesion
> **Level** mixed ability
> **Time** 15–20 minutes

Procedure

1 Students finish the sentence *I don't like people who* … in as many ways as they possibly can.
2 Students stand and mingle. They talk to classmates and try to find other students with the same dislikes.

3 When they do find students whose dislike matches their own, they explain to each other why they have such a dislike.
4 In plenary, volunteers tell the class about anything that they learned or that surprised them in the exchange with other students.

Optional follow-up
Students write a paragraph explaining their dislike.

6.19 Careers in my family

    Aim   fluency practice, individual expression, class cohesion
    Level mixed ability
    Time   15–20 minutes

Procedure

1 In small groups, students take turns giving three minute talks about their father's occupation; their mother's occupation; and their own present or future career.
2 Each group chooses its best presentation to give to the whole class.
3 Volunteers ask questions.
4 The whole class talks about whether a person's career choice is influenced by one's family.

6.20 What we want from our work

    Aim   fluency practice, individual expression, class cohesion
    Level intermediate–advanced
    Time   15–20 minutes

Procedure

1 In small groups, students brainstorm for what people want from their jobs/careers. (See Box 74 for suggestions.)
2 With the whole class, create a blackboard list.
3 Each group arranges the suggestions in order of preference – from what is most important to what is least important.
4 Volunteers tell the class about their own personal most important career want.

Box 74 Suggested list of what people want from their careers

- Money
- Prestige
- Friends
- Interesting things to do
- Pleasant work place
- Opportunity for advancement
- Challenges
- Chance to be helpful
- Chance to add meaning to life
- Chance to be creative
- Chance to travel
- Chance to meet interesting people
- Chance for adventure
- Possibility to be creative
- Job security
- Lots of vacations
- Flexible working hours
- A sympathetic boss

6.21 Our own good folder

Aim	reading, individual work
Level	all levels
Time	fluid

Procedure

1 Each student has his own 'good folder' which he/she brings to class every day. In the folder there are any interesting stories, poems, or exercises, games that the student considers good things to do when there is time.
2 When students have some extra time after an activity, send them to their own 'good folder' for work.
3 Periodically, when you are doing something that students are enjoying but that you don't have time to finish, suggest it for their 'good folder'.

Notes
- Occasionally, have volunteers share something from their 'good folder' with the class.
- When you find something interesting, like a particularly clever cartoon, offer it for students to put in their 'good folders'.

6.22 Words on my desk

Aim   vocabulary review

Level   all levels

Time   fluid

Procedure

1 Occasionally ask students to write ten words that they have come across lately and really want to learn properly on a list.
2 They tape this list to a visible spot on their desk.
3 As you circulate in the room ask students questions about the words. Examples: *Where did you see this word? Can you look up and spell this word? Do you know what this word means? Can you use this word in a sentence?*

6.23 Drawing interpretation

Aim   fluency practice, reading comprehension, reading interpretation, class cohesion

Level   all levels

Time   fluid

Procedure

1 After you have finished reading a poem, story, essay, book, or article, ask students to do a quick drawing of what they consider to be the central or most important idea of the reading.
2 In small groups each student holds up his/her picture while the other students interpret the picture.
3 The student who drew the picture tells the others what he/she had in mind and what he/she might have learned from them.

4 The whole group talks about the meaning of the reading and how it might have changed for them as they looked and talked about the pictures.

Notes

- Some students may protest that they don't know how to draw. For them, demonstrate with some stick figures, or lines and circles to show them that you don't expect artistry.
- This activity works best if you set a time limit of no more than three minutes for the drawing.

7 Making students responsible for their own learning

It happened in the first grade. The teacher was explaining to her new students that they would be doing something called *Show and Tell*. Students would bring something that was dear to them from home, and tell their classmates about their special object. That way, a piece of home would come to school, and school wouldn't seem like such a strange place.

'Miss Smith,' said little Tommy eagerly. 'Can I bring my dog, Rickie?'

'No, Tommy, I'm afraid not,' said Miss Smith. 'I did say that you should bring a **thing** from home, didn't I? Now a doggie is not a thing. A dog is an animal, and we don't allow animals from home to come to school, do we?'

'But Miss Smith,' said Tommy. 'I have taught Rickie how to whistle.'

Now Miss Smith was truly intrigued – a whistling dog – well, that would be quite something. So she gave her permission.

Well, the next day, Tommy showed up with Rickie. And what a cute dog Rickie was – all white and fluffy, he sat on the teacher's desk and looked happily at the children as he wagged his tail, **but he did not whistle.**

'What is this, Tommy?' said the disappointed teacher. 'I thought you said that you had taught your dog how to whistle.'

'Well, yes,' responded the ever resourceful Tommy. 'I said that I had **taught** him how to whistle. I didn't say that he had **learned!**'

Teaching, of course, ultimately depends on the willingness of the student to learn: unless the learner takes some responsibility in the shape of active cooperation and effort, there will be no learning in spite of the efforts of excellent teachers. The realization that students must be responsible for their own learning is perhaps most applicable in the large multilevel class. In these classes, teachers cannot always know whether their assignments are useful for all students, and whether all students are making sufficient progress. It is then up to the students to monitor their own progress and to help the teacher and fellow students to notice where and how they need help. Good learners, like good teachers, are unique. We all approach learning in our own special ways. The way we learn is connected to our built-in habits, our state of motivation, our moods, and our needs. In the normal way, all of us learn our first language, and, although some people do seem to have more of a talent for language learning, I am convinced that we are all quite capable of learning other languages. A lot simply depends on how much we need that language and how much energy we are willing to invest in learning it. At any rate, it is quite clear that learning a language is just as much, if not more, the work of the student as it is the work of the teacher. Our classrooms will doubtless function better if our students realize that while the teacher can indeed help them, motivate them, and make their learning more interesting, in the final analysis they, themselves, are very much responsible for their own learning. The greatest teacher in the universe will not make the new language theirs, unless they personally put in the effort, take the risks, and exert the energy involved in language learning.

Here are some ideas that will help your students to focus more clearly on their own learning:

- Before a test, give out sample questions, asking students to work on these in small groups and to discuss their ideas with the whole class.
- At the start of your course, elicit student concerns about language learning and about this course in particular.
- Allow students to create study guides before a test.
- Have students write their expectations of the course.

The activities in this chapter will help to make students aware of their own language learning potential, monitor their own progress, and take responsibility for their own learning.

7.1 What kind of a learner am I?

Aim   self-discovery, fluency practice, writing

Level   mixed ability

Time   15–20 minutes

Preparation Put the following list of statements on the board or make enough handouts so that each small group in your class will have one.

- Some of us learn best through our eyes.
- Some of us learn best through our ears.
- Some of us need to write something down to learn it.
- Some of us have to associate an old thing with a new thing.
- Some of us need to repeat something many times.

- Some of us need to use the new knowledge with people.
- Some of us need music to learn.
- Some of us need to walk around or move to learn.

Procedure

1 Write three words that your students don't know on the board. Let's say the words are *summit*, *generous*, and *joyful*. Give them the meanings of the words: *the top or the highest point, willing to give, and very happy*. Tell students that you will give them a few minutes to make these words their own and that later you will want to know how they did it.

2 In small groups, students talk about how they went about learning the meanings. A secretary in each group summarizes the various learning styles and strategies.

3 A spokesperson from each group talks about what students did to learn the new words. As they speak, they should also check items on the list you have given them and add new items if they come up.

4 Say *Jose, you said that you learn best when you write things down. Can you explain why?* Get several individual explanations from volunteers.

5 Ask students if they would learn the words differently if they had more time and could do so at home.

6 Explain that we all learn in different ways, and that it is important to know which is the best way for us. Sometimes, it can be useful to switch learning styles. We may discover that by switching styles we can learn something that we were not able to learn before.

7 Students write a short composition called *My Style of Learning*. They file the composition in their folder (see activity 4.15).

8 At the end of the course, they may wish to add something to this composition or to change it.

7.2 Setting goals for myself

Aim   clarification of language goals, fluency practice, writing

Level   intermediate–advanced

Time   30–45 minutes

Procedure

1 Students write down a personal or a professional goal they have set for themselves.
2 They talk about this goal with a partner.
3 Students write down a language goal that they have for the next six months.
4 In small groups, students talk about their language goals.
5 Students write down a language goal they have for the coming week.
6 They share this goal with a partner.
7 With the same partner, students talk about various ways in which they can accomplish their goals. They should write a series of steps. For example: *I plan to learn five new words every day. I plan to watch television every night. I plan to speak with native speakers.*
8 Volunteers speak about their personal goals.
9 Students write a short composition about A *language goal I have for this week and how I can reach it.*
10 Students file their composition in their language folder to be read and commented on at the end of the week.
11 At the end of the week, volunteers talk about whether and/or how they were able to fulfill their goals for the week.

7.3   How a teacher helped me

Aim	fluency practice, writing, clarifying commitments
Level	mixed level
Time	20–30 minutes
Preparation	Think of the various ways in which teachers have helped you, and be prepared to share this with students. (See Box 75 for suggestions.)

Procedure

1 Share your helpful teacher stories with the class.
2 In small groups, students exchange helpful teacher stories.
3 Each group chooses its most interesting story and writes it up.
4 The stories are posted on the wall of the classroom and students walk about reading and commenting on the stories.

Box 75 How a teacher helped me

- The best teacher I had never checked homework. She said it was our business whether we did it or not. It was the first time I started doing homework.
- The best teacher I had always listened to me when I had problems, and then she made me think of ways I should solve those problems.
- The best teacher I had told funny jokes and made me forget that I sat in class. I learned so many words from his jokes.
- The best teacher I had made me think and that made me want to learn more.
- The best teacher I had made me think that I was smart and that I could accomplish something. She called on me very often and made me feel special.

7.4 How can the teacher help me?

Aim fluency practice, writing,

Level mixed level

Time 20–30 minutes

Procedure

1 Brainstorm with the class for ways in which a teacher can help students and ways in which a teacher cannot help. Ask secretaries from the class to write suggestions on the board. (See Box 76 for suggestions.)
2 In small groups, students talk about specific ways in which they would like the teacher to help them.
3 Each group creates a wish list for the teacher.
4 Collect these wish lists and promise that you will consider them in your teaching.
5 Periodically during the term refer to certain wish lists as you do an activity or a presentation.

Box 76 Suggestions on what the teacher can and cannot do

What can the teacher do?
- Explain clearly
- Write clearly on the board
- Explain the rules of grammar
- Give assignments
- Make the lessons interesting
- Check my homework

What the teacher cannot do
- Make me listen
- Make me do my assignments
- Make me participate in class
- Make me interested
- Make me progress in language learning

7.5   How I can help myself

Aim   fluency practice, writing, clarifying commitments
Level mixed level
Time   20–30 minutes

Procedure

1 With the class, brainstorm for ways in which students can help themselves to become better learners. Ask student secretaries to write the suggestions up on the board as they appear. (See Box 77 for possible suggestions.)
2 Each student commits to practice one of the suggestions during the next few lessons. They write their commitment in a contract. (See Box 78 for an example.)
3 A few lessons later, ask students to go back to their commitment and, in small groups, talk to classmates about how they went about working on the suggestion.

Note

The procedure can be repeated several times during the semester.

Box 77 Suggestions on how students can improve their own learning

- I can listen better.
- I can look up more words in the dictionary and write them on my cards.
- I can go to more movies.
- I can read more books. I learn a lot from children's stories.
- I can get a roommate who is a native speaker.
- I can talk more to my landlady.
- I can talk more to tourists who speak the target language.
- I can go over my cards more often.
- I can do my homework better.
- I can talk more in class.
- I can ask the teacher more questions.

Box 78 Example of a commitment contract

Student's Name ....
During the next few lessons I commit to
- doing my homework
- reading more out loud
- reviewing my vocabulary every day

Signed .... Date ....

7.6 Personal conferences

Aim | fluency practice, goal clarification, getting to know students' needs, giving students the opportunity to think about their own learning

Level | mixed ability

Time | fluid

Preparation | Set aside a few longer lessons during the term when the class will do a written project while you meet each student individually to talk about that student's progress. Give each student a period of seven to ten minutes. Prepare a set of questions for the conference and let students have the questions prior to the conference. (See Box 79 for suggestions.)

Procedure

1 Explain that conferences are there to let the students tell you about their own progress and what they have been doing to help themselves to learn the new language.
2 Give out the conference questionnaire, go over it and ask if there are questions.
3 Early in the session, set conference dates and give every student his/her appointed time.
4 During the conference, allow the student plenty of talking time, and if possible take notes.
5 File the notes away, and refer to them whenever you are dealing with that student. You will find these notes very helpful.

Box 79 Possible questions to use during a conference

- Why are you studying the new language?
- What do you find easiest in learning the language?
- What do you find most difficult?
- What do you do to help yourself make progress?
- What do you enjoy most in our class?
- What could other students do to help you?
- What could you do to help other students?
- What can the teacher do to help you?

7.7   What kind of a listener am I?

Aim	improving listening skills
Level	intermediate–advanced
Time	fluid

Preparation   If you have a video of a film and have access to TV/VCR equipment, have it ready (any film will do). If you don't have any such equipment, use any short interesting reading.

Procedure

1 Together with students, make a blackboard list of times when listening is important. (See Box 80 for suggestions.)
2 In small groups, students talk about what they can do to improve their listening skills. Listen to reports from groups and write the suggestions up on the board. (See Box 81 for suggestions.)
3 Ask for a show of hands, when you ask *Who does this?* about various activities on the blackboard list.
4 Ask *Is there a suggestion here about something you haven't yet done to improve your listening but you could start doing?*
5 In pairs, students talk about how they could improve their listening skills.

Optional follow-up

- Play the opening scene of the film you have brought with the TV set turned around so that the students can't see the film.
- In small groups, students decide what the scene was about. Speakers from each group report.
- Ask *What were the clues (hints) that told you what this was about?*
- Play the scene again in the same way.
- In small groups, students decide whether they have changed their minds about anything.
- Play the scene again, this time with both sight and sound. Students will be very happy if they predicted correctly and surprised if they did not. Analyze the language of the scene by noting the words that either gave correct or incorrect clues.

Variation

If you don't have TV/VCR equipment, you can read a story out loud with your back to the class, and after the second reading, have them look at the text.

Box 80 When listening is important

- When someone gives you directions on how to get to their house on the phone.
- When watching a movie or a TV program.
- When listening to the weather report.
- When listening to a restaurant server telling you what is on the menu.
- In class.
- During a lecture.
- When announcements are given – in school, at the airport, in a bus station.
- When the doctor tells you what medicines to take and when to take them.
- When you get directions.
- During a physical education lesson, when an instructor is telling you what to do.
- When listening to telephone messages.
- When you call up to find out about films.
- When a lawyer explains a contract to you.
- When your landlord tells you about the rules of the apartment.

Box 81 Suggestions for improving listening

- Ask people to please repeat.
- Listen to news programs when you already know the news.
- Re-play your telephone messages several times.
- Go to films that you have already seen with subtitles in your own language.
- For listening to lectures, learn transition words like *First, second, third, the important point is, moreover, to clarify, in conclusion*.
- Watch TV programs about material that you are familiar with.
- Listen to the way people in restaurants or on the bus talk.
- Listen to tourists who speak the native language.
- Listen to songs several times and try to write the words down.
- Get some good book listening tapes from the library and listen to them when you exercise.

7.8 This course will be a success for me if ...

Aim fluency practice, considering course goals, analysis of learning needs, writing

Level mixed levels

Time 15–20 minutes

Procedure

1 Ask everyone to take out a small piece of paper.
2 Dictate while students write *This course will become a success for me if ...* .
3 Students finish the sentence in any way they wish.
4 Collect all the papers in a bag.
5 Students pull a paper from the bag. If they happen to pull out their own, they should put it back.
6 Students write a comment or reaction to the idea on the piece of paper they have found and put their initials under their comment.
7 They put the paper back, pull another piece from the bag and repeat the procedure.
8 Keep this going as long as interest seems high and until every student has had a chance to make some comments on the papers of other students.
9 Take the bag home and note what students see as a successful course.
10 Report to students on some interesting things you learned and periodically remind them of their ideas of success.

7.9 What kind of a reader am I?

Aim reading

Level mixed ability

Time fluid

Preparation Bring a children's picture book.

Procedure

1 Ask *When you are about to go on a long bus or train trip and you want to buy a book in your own language that will amuse you during the entire trip, how do you go about choosing such a book?*

2 In small groups, students list ways in which they choose their books.
3 With the help of a secretary, make a list of their reasons on the board. (See Box 82 for suggestions.) If some of the items on the list have not been mentioned by the students, add them to the board list.
4 Show the class some of the pictures in the children's book you have brought, and have them guess the content.
5 Read brief parts of the book from randomly selected places, and again ask for guesses about content.
6 If possible, read the entire book to verify student guesses.
7 Talk with the class about the pre-reading strategies you used (talking about reasons for choosing a reading; looking at pictures to predict reading; glancing through content to note what the book is about). Note that such techniques are helpful in reading any text.

Optional follow-up

- Either individually or in small groups, students look at a difficult reading in their textbook, or one that you provide. They use as many of the strategies listed on the board as possible before they begin the reading.
- As a whole class, talk about which strategies they used.
- Assign the reading, with comprehension questions, either for class or for home reading.
- Talk about whether and how the pre-reading strategies helped.

Note

Encourage students to use these pre-reading strategies in their future reading assignments.

Box 82 Suggestions for how books are chosen

- I get books that friends recommend.
- I read the review on the back of the book to try to decide whether I will like this book.
- I read the first page.
- I look through the names of the chapters.
- I look at the table of contents.
- I look at the pictures.
- I look at the first line/paragraph in each chapter.
- I read the beginning and the ending.

7.10 Am I brave enough?

Aim   encouraging risk-taking. (See Box 83 for a definition of language risk-taking.)

Level   mixed ability

Time   10–15 minutes

Procedure

1 On the board write *A good language learner must be a risk-taker.*
2 In small groups, students make lists of what they consider language risk-taking. (See Box 84 for suggestions.)
3 Spokespersons from the groups offer suggestions, and with the help of a secretary, compile a class list on the board.
4 In pairs, students talk about whether they have taken sufficient risks and how they could become better risk-takers.

Optional follow-up

Students write about a recent language risk-taking experience.

Box 83 Definition of language risk-taking

Risk-taking in a language means that you are willing to use your hunch about what the right language should be, and are willing to take the chance on using language a bit beyond your present ability. This is not always easy as a language risk-taker may well be laughed at, or met with blank stares. Risk-taking sometimes involves guessing at the correct form or the pronunciation. A certain amount of risk-taking is necessary in language acquisition, and willing risk-takers are, as a rule, good language learners.

Box 84 Suggestions on how to become a risk-taker

- Talk to native speakers every chance you get.
- Ask questions when you don't understand something.
- Use a new word as soon as you have learned it.

- Go to the theater even when you think that you won't understand everything.
- Write letters to the editor in the target language newspaper.
- Start conversations at parties.
- Ask for directions.
- Give directions.
- Get a job that requires the use of the target language.
- Ask for help with your pronunciation.
- Ask for help with your spelling.
- Look up words in a monolingual target dictionary.
- Read newspapers and magazines in the target language.
- Read a favorite author translated into the target language.

7.11 Question posters

Aim	repetition of frequently used phrases, fluency practice, helping students practice the words they will actually need in class
Level	beginners
Time	fluid
Preparation	Bring large paper and felt markers.

Procedure

1 Ask the class to help you think of expressions that they often need both in class and outside of class. (See Box 85 for suggestions.)
2 Write their suggestions and your own additions on the board.
3 In small groups, students choose one or two of these and create decorative posters.
4 Place the posters on the walls around the room and point to them every time one is needed.

Note

This activity works well because the language is both created and needed by the student.

Box 85 Commonly used expressions

- Please.
- Thank you.
- How are you?
- I am fine, thank you.
- Excuse me.
- Where is ... ?

- Where are ... ?
- How do we say ... ?
- How do you spell ... ?
- Can you tell me how to ... ?
- I don't know how ...
- How much is this?

Note

The same system can be used for learning transitional expressions, difficult words in a domain, prepositional verbs, or irregular verbs.

7.12 How do I catch and correct my own mistakes?

Aim self-correction, fluency practice
Level mixed ability
Time fluid

Procedure

1 Write on the board *I keep making the same mistakes over and over again.*
2 Ask *How many people agree with what I wrote on the board?*
3 Get a show of hands.
4 In pairs, students talk about their most frequent mistakes and ask their partners for help in spotting and correcting them.
5 Ask *Did anyone get any good advice?*
6 With the help of a secretary, get a list of suggestions up on the board and add your own ideas to the list. (See Box 86 for suggestions.)
7 In pairs, students decide which suggestions might work for them.
8 In subsequent lessons ask if they are making progress in correcting their own mistakes.

Box 86 Spotting and correcting our mistakes

- Ask a competent speaker of English to work with you on a sound and then record yourself making that sound. Practice the sound often and listen to yourself.
- With the help of a native speaker, change an incorrect expression to a correct one and write the correct one in a place where you will often see it. Use it often.
- Write words that you misspell on small cards and post the cards above your bathroom mirror. As you comb your hair, write these words in the air.
- Try to associate the spelling of a word with something you know.
- Say words that are difficult to pronounce ten times every morning – monitor yourself carefully for correction.
- Try to think of words that you do know how to pronounce that are close in sound to those that you don't know.
- When you hear a TV announcer saying a word that you have a hard time with, say it many times just the way the announcer said it.

7.13 Instant answers

Aim	self-correction
Level	mixed ability
Time	fluid
Preparation	Write up a short answer quiz. Fold back the bottom of the paper and write the answers to all the questions under the fold. Make enough copies for your students.

Procedure

1 Students do the quiz individually.
2 They compare their answers with a partner.
3 They open the fold to see how many answers they got right.

Variation

You can also write the answers under a large piece of paper on the board and remove the paper for a check once everyone has finished working with a partner.

7.14 Words from the world

Aim vocabulary practice
Level intermediate–advanced
Time fluid

Procedure

1 Students bring in new words that they have heard or seen somewhere outside of class.
2 Take no more than five such words each lesson.
3 Write the words on the board. If students remember where they heard these, try to associate the word with the context.
4 Explain the words or elicit explanations from students.
5 Ask the class to offer suggestions on how the words should be learned.
6 Write up a list of suggestions, and have the class vote on the best two. Use these!

Note

My favorite is to have students, in small groups, create little skits that include the new words.

7.15 Questions on a stick

Aim question formations, reading, speaking
Level intermediate–advanced
Time fluid
Preparation Bring in, for each student, a flat stick (the kind that go into ice-cream bars are perfect, or you could use straight pieces of sturdy cardboard cut into straight sticks).

Procedure

1 Students write their own names on the sticks.
2 Collect the sticks in a jar and keep the jar on your desk.
3 Each student writes out a question on a topic recently read about.
4 A volunteer goes to the front of the class and reads his/her question.

5 Then he/she pulls a stick from the jar, and reads out the name of the student who will answer the question.
6 If the student whose name was read cannot answer the question, the volunteer repeats the question and pulls another stick.
7 Repeat a third time if the answer was not successfully answered.
8 Allow anyone else to answer.
9 The student who has answered successfully becomes the next volunteer.

Caveat: Be sure that you don't reverse steps 4 and 5. The whole idea here is that everyone has to be ready to answer because no one knows whose name is going to be pulled.

7.16 Many ways to be smart

Aim	speaking, listening, analysis of personal intelligence
Level	intermediate–advanced
Time	fluid

Preparation On the walls in your classroom post the following, each on a different piece of paper:

Verbal ability
Enjoying work with words in any language. Writers, poets, journalists, speakers, and actors are good at this.

Logical/mathematical ability
Liking to work with numbers, patterns, or categories. Scientists, researchers, engineers, mathematicians, and accountants are good at this.

Visual/spatial ability
Good at finding your way in new places. Being able to manipulate images. Decorators, artists, and engineers are good at this.

Physical ability
The ability to use your body well like dancers or athletes do.

Musical ability
Loving and knowing how to recognize music.

Social ability
Being able to get along well with all kinds of people.

Procedure

1 Talk with your class about the different talents and abilities people possess. Point out those that are posted on the walls, but allow students to contribute others.
2 Students walk about the room and stand under the ability that pertains most to them.
3 They talk with other students of the same ability and explain why they know this about themselves.
4 Students find someone from a different ability and explain their choices to each other.
5 Talk with the whole class about how your special ability can help you to study a language. (See Box 87 for suggestions.)

Box 87 Suggestions for how one's special ability can help with language learning

- Verbal ability – write poems with new words, think of silly stories with words, compare and contrast words to each other, use new words often
- Logical/mathematical ability – create patterns for new grammar rules and new vocabulary; arrange new words in a logical sequence
- Visual ability – draw pictures of words, create unusual spaces for new words
- Musical ability – make up songs with new sentences and new words; play music while you study
- Physical ability – move around when you study, give a physical exercise a name in the new language

7.17 Grade contracts

Aim	fluency practice, writing, class organization
Level	intermediate–advanced
Time	10–15 minutes

Preparation Prepare sample grade contracts for your students. (See Box 88 for suggestions.)

Procedure

1 Talk with students about the meaning of grades. Ask if grades are important to them and why. Ask them to help you formulate what the requirements for the grades A, B, and C should be. Explain that A means outstanding, B means good, and C means average.
2 Tell students what you hope that they will accomplish in order to earn each grade.
3 In small groups, students brainstorm for suggestions for what they think would be outstanding work, good work, or average work. Listen to the suggestions of each group and, if appropriate, incorporate their suggestions into your own.
4 Explain that in order to receive the appropriate contract grade, it is not enough to just do the work but that the work also has to be of high quality, and that you will work together to create self-evaluation forms to help them decide if they have done quality work. (See the next activity.)
5 Students choose one of the contracts you have been working on. They copy it and sign it.
6 Collect the contracts and keep them until the end of the term. Then, give them back to students and ask them to decide whether they have fulfilled the obligations of the contract or perhaps even exceeded their own expectations.

Box 88 Examples of contracts

Name of student ....

Today's date ....

To receive a grade of C in this course I will:
- Come to class each day (no unexcused absences)
- Participate in class discussions
- Do the daily assignments
- Do the short speeches
- Do the midterm review
- **Receive at least C on all my quizzes**
- Receive at least C on my final

Signed ....

To receive a grade of B in this course I will:
- Come to class each day (no unexcused absences)
- Participate in class discussions
- Do the daily assignments
- Do the short speeches
- Do the midterm review
- **Receive at least B on all my quizzes**
- Receive at least B on my final
- Read and report on three articles provided by the instructor

Signed ....

To receive a grade of A in this course I will:
- Come to class each day (no unexcused absences)
- Participate in class discussions
- Do the daily assignments
- Do the short speeches
- Do the midterm review
- **Receive an A on almost all my quizzes**
- Receive an A on my final
- Read and report on three articles provided by the instructor
- Do the special project

Signed ....

7.18 Self-check forms

Aim	self-evaluation, reading, setting standards
Level	intermediate–advanced
Time	20–30 minutes

Preparation Decide exactly what you want students to accomplish in their work and put this on the self-evaluation form. (See Box 89 for an example.)

Procedure

1 Read through the evaluation form with students.
2 Give them an example of the kind of project you want to evaluate. (See Box 90 for an example.)
3 Ask for additional student suggestions and if appropriate add them to your own.
4 In small groups, students study the composition and evaluate it according to the evaluation form.
5 Spokespersons for the groups report their conclusions to the whole class.
6 Invite comments and reactions from the class.

Box 89 Check form for a composition

- Does your composition have a title?
- Is the first paragraph a good introduction? How could it be improved?
- Is the composition divided into paragraphs?
- Do all the ideas in each paragraph belong together?
- Do the details support the main ideas?
- Is the composition interesting?
- How could it be made more interesting?
- Is the use of language appropriate?
- Does the composition have a good conclusion?
- How could it be improved?

Box 90 Composition to be evaluated

My Wonderful Mother

My mother is the nicest person I know. She is very pretty and only 40 years old everybody thinks that she my sister.

My mother can do many things. She has long black hair and she knows how to cook very good food. She also knows to sing and she has nice time with me and my brother even if she must to work very hardly every day in my father's story. My mother came from Japan when she little girl, nine years old and she can still speak the Japan language and also Spanish and now she to learn English, because I learn English.

Next week my mother comes to visit me here in Arizona. I want to make her very happy. I will bring her to class with me — O.K. Teacher?

Evaluation

- Does your composition have a title? Yes.
- Is the first paragraph a good introduction? So, so – could be a lot better.
- How could it be improved? Add more details – why is your mother so nice? what makes her pretty? how do you feel when everyone thinks that she is your sister?
- Is the composition divided into paragraphs? Yes.
- Do all the ideas in each paragraph belong together? No, the second paragraph has many ideas that belong in the first paragraph and some ideas that could make different paragraphs.
- Do the details support the main ideas? No – the main idea of paragraph two is that mother can do many things, but some of the sentences don't talk about that.
- Is the composition interesting? Yes, but it could be more interesting.
- How could it be made more interesting? Concentrate more on one thing. Tell us more about what she does with you and your brother, or in another paragraph tell us about how she came to America.
- Is the use of language appropriate? There are some mistakes – *story* instead of *store* and she works *hard* and not *hardly*.
- Does the composition have a good conclusion? No.
- How could it be improved? You need a better summary or concluding sentence.

8 Establishing routines and procedures

In the large class, it is important that rules of conduct, policies, routines, and procedures be set up and followed in a fairly predictable manner. It is important that students know how and when they will be evaluated, what the attendance policy of the class is, how homework is checked, what the syllabus of the course is, how they are supposed to conduct themselves, and what level of achievement is expected from them. Well-established routines give students a sense of stability and security. Once such routines are functioning properly, instructions need not be repeated as often, student responsibility increases and the entire process of teaching and learning works more smoothly.

I have found that my classes operate better if I incorporate students in the rule-making process by stating my outlook, asking for comments and suggestions, accepting compromises and then formulating the rules and posting them in a prominent spot on the classroom wall. This does not mean, of course, that rules are never broken. As I have stated before, rules are there to guide us, not necessarily to bind us. When I do break a class rule to accommodate a student, I try to do it with a smile and with the permission of the class. The main idea is to plant the notion that we – the teachers – are not police officers. **Rather, it is up to each individual student to observe how he/she measures up to expectations and possibly is an example for other students.**

One of our most significant principles in large class management is to create a climate where students will feel safe and where they will perceive other students as partners in the process of learning rather than competitors on the success scale.

I have found the following ideas helpful in setting up classroom rituals and routines in the large multilevel class:

- Write out the day's activities on the board before the class arrives and check off the activities as the lesson progresses. If you have the use of an overhead projector, write out the program on a transparency. That way you can use it again in a parallel class. (See activity 8.4 for clarification.)
- Keep three to five cards on your desk to write yourself reminders about various students as you walk around the class.
- Post deadlines on when things are due in a visible place in the classroom.

- Assign 'paper persons' to collect and distribute papers.
- Practice the 'three before me' rule – that is to say, when working in groups, students should ask three classmates an information question before they turn to you.
- Practice repeated class rituals. (See activities 8.7–8.11.)
- Prepare as many handouts as you possibly can get ready before the beginning of your course and make a course packet for your students.
- Have a set of extra pencils and extra paper on your desk for those students who invariably forget.
- On the first day of class ask students to write their names on clothes pins (pegs). Attach these to a rope between two chairs at the entrance of the class. As students enter class, they find their own pin and put it on your desk. The remaining pins will be the students who are absent.

The activities of this chapter should prove helpful in the development of useful routines.

8.1   Introducing the class syllabus

Aim	reading, understanding personal and class goals, fluency practice
Level	intermediate–advanced
Time	20–30 minutes
Preparation	Write out your anticipated syllabus for the course. Try to make it as realistic as possible. It should include your approximate weekly plan, the material you hope to cover during the course, what will be expected of students, the books you will use, and your procedure for grading. See Box 91 for a sample syllabus in an eight-week course.

Procedure

1 On the first day of class, after you have greeted students, read their names and followed some of the introductory activities suggested in the early chapters, ask students to anticipate what will be happening in your class.
2 In small groups, students talk about and ask a secretary to write down their expectations.
3 A spokesperson from each group reports on the group's expectations. A secretary, with your help, summarizes these and writes them on the board.

4 Validate the expectations by pointing out those which indeed will match your syllabus. Express happy surprise at others that you have not considered but consider valuable, and say that you will try to incorporate these into your syllabus.
5 Explain that a syllabus is a tentative outline of study that is meant to guide us but is flexible and can be changed when needed.
6 Give out the syllabus.
7 Students read the syllabus and note where and how it mirrors their expectations. Spokespersons from the groups report the group findings. Promise to look over all student suggestions and to incorporate as many as possible.
8 Let the class know which suggestions you have decided to incorporate.

Box 91 A sample syllabus for an eight-week advanced reading class

General Statement: In this class, we will work on improving our reading and comprehension ability by reading and talking about both short and long texts. We see every member of the class both as a learner and a teacher. In this class, you should use classmates as people who can help you learn or whom you can help to learn.

Your instructor is ....

I would like for you to call me ....

You can reach me at ....

My office hours are ....
Please come and see me during my office hours. That's what they are for. I am always happy to see you and to hear about your progress. Part of my job is to help you with any problems you might have.

The textbook we will be using is ....

It is available at ....

In addition to the short readings in our textbook, we will be reading the novel .... by

....

It is available at ....

What you will be expected to do:
- The daily assignments
- Short speeches on topics given by the instructor, or topics that you choose
- weekly dictations
- weekly quizzes
- intensive class readings
- extensive readings in your novel

Here is how your grade will be decided:

$\frac{1}{3}$ class attendance, participation, and daily projects

$\frac{1}{3}$ tests, quizzes, and group reviews

$\frac{1}{3}$ your special project

Study plan:

Week one: Introduction to the class and to other students. Chapters 1 and 2 in our text.

Week two: Introduction to your special project. Chapter 3 in our text.

Week three: Start of weekly dictations and weekly quizzes. Introduction to the novel. Chapter 4 in our text.

Week four: Chapters 1, 2, 3 in the novel. Chapter 5 in the text.

Week five: Chapters 4–8 in the novel. Midterm group review. (See activity 3.4.)

Week six: Chapters 9–11 in the novel. Chapter 6 in the text.

Week seven: Your special project is due. Chapters 12–15 in the novel. Chapter 7 in the text.

Week eight: Conclusion of the novel. Chapter 8 in the text. Final exam.

8.2 Setting up the class calendar

Aim	class organization, fluency practice, reading
Level	all levels
Time	10–15 minutes
Preparation	Make a large calendar that can be seen by the whole class. Attach a pencil and eraser to it.

Procedure

1 Pass a small version of the calendar around the room. On it you will have marked test and quiz dates as well as any holidays or dates when the class will not meet. If you are planning any kind of special student presentations during the term, ask students to write their names in the appropriate squares on the calendars, making sure that there are no more than three special presentations on a given day. Students should also write in their birthday date if it happens to fall at any time during the course.

2 In small groups, students talk about the value of planning a calendar. Below are some of the issues they might want to consider:

  – Do you keep a personal calendar? Why or why not?
  – Do you think that people today are too busy?
  – Are certain cultures too concerned with time?
  – Is it important to be on time for all meetings?

  Listen to reports from all groups, and with the whole class talk about the value of a class calendar.

3 After class, check what the students have written, make any re-adjustments needed (for example, there might be more than three students written down on a speech day).

4 Make a copy of the completed calendar for each of your students and transfer all the information to the large calendar in front of the class.

8.3 Checking homework, tardiness, and attendance

Aim	to register attendance, tardiness, and homework; to have students express themselves clearly and concisely
Level	all levels
Time	fluid
Preparation	On a sheet of paper, write as a heading the name of the class and the date. Divide the paper into three columns with the following titles: *Name, Time, Homework*.

Procedure

1 Explain the sheet to the class, including what they have to fill in under each column: their name, the time when they arrived at the

lesson, comments on their homework (see the notes below).

2 Have another sheet posted at the door for latecomers. They should also note the time they arrived and a reason for their lateness.

3 Pass the paper around the class so that students can fill in the appropriate slots.

4 You can keep these papers in a folder as your attendance record, or you can transfer the information into your attendance book.

Notes

- The procedure eliminates the need for taking attendance and for changing notation for latecomers. Students' self-registry promotes feelings of responsibility and self-discipline.

- When you first explain the procedure to your class, you might discuss with them appropriate 'homework comments'. Possibilities are:
  • finished and did a good job
  • didn't have time to finish
  • did everything except the third question
  • didn't understand what to do
  • couldn't do it – personal reasons

8.4 The daily plan

Aim	reading, review
Level	all levels
Time	fluid
Preparation	Before each lesson, write a brief outline of your lesson plan on the board. Try to write the plan in the same place each day.

Procedure

1 At the beginning of each lesson, go over the day's plan with students.

2 As the lesson progresses, check off the items that have been covered.

3 As the lesson draws to a close, ask students to briefly review the points that have been covered, and note which items you added or did not get around to doing.

4 Ask the student who is writing the 'absent student notebook' (see next activity) to make a note of the items you want to cover during the next lesson.

8.5 The absent student notebook

Aim	writing, homework reminder, review
Level	all levels
Time	fluid
Preparation	Prepare a loose-leaf notebook with paper.

Procedure

1 Each week appoint a different student to write up the page for students who have been absent. Be sure to put the notebook in some obvious spot where students will see it.
2 The appointed student copies your daily plan from the blackboard, and checks off all the activities that have been done, makes notes on any handouts that have been given out and all the assignments given for the next lesson.
3 Place all handouts in the back pocket of the notebook or in an easily accessible place.
4 Students who have been absent check the book to make up assignments.

8.6 Exit notes

Aim	writing, self-analysis, building of a cohesive classroom environment
Level	all levels
Time	5–10 minutes

Procedure

1 At the end of some lessons, ask students to write you a note summarizing what they have learned during the lesson. Prompt them to consider all four skills, that is: *What did we do for speaking? reading? listening? writing during this lesson?*
2 Students first write on their own.
3 Collect the notes as students exit.
4 Use the notes to check what students know and what needs to be reviewed and use this in future lessons.

Optional follow-up

In small groups, students tell one another what they have written. They may add or expand on their individual note after they have talked with classmates.

Class rituals

Class rituals are special learning routines that are done regularly: some in every lesson, some not. Unlike the routines in the first part of this chapter, these rituals have nothing to do with actual classroom or lesson management. Rather, they are simply regular learning activities providing a set of structured mini-discourses that students can practice and become experts in. The familiarity and predictability of these routines promotes a feeling of security.

8.7 Lesson starters

    Aim   building of a cohesive classroom environment, fluency practice, vocabulary expansion
    Level all levels
    Time 10–15 minutes

Procedure

1 Begin your class by talking about the weather. Ask *What's the weather today?* For suggestions of other starters at different levels, see Box 92.
2 Make sure that the class knows appropriate vocabulary such as *hot, cold, sunny, rainy, cloudy.*
3 Ask for weather around the world by pointing to a map.

Note

This activity works very well in an international framework where students enjoy telling one another about the weather situation in their own countries.

Box 92 Suggestions for starters

For beginner students
- *What day is today? What day was it yesterday? What day will it be tomorrow?*
- *How are you? I am fine. And you? I am fine too.* Practice first chorally and then in pairs and as a mingling activity.

For intermediate students
- Begin with *How are you today?* and ask students to rate their well-being on a scale of one to ten. In a mingling activity, students share their number with classmates and explain the reason why they feel as they do.
- Put a set of adjectives, such as *tired, hungry, excited, happy, enthusiastic*, and *interested* on the board and ask students to choose the one that best describes them at the moment. In a mingling activity, students share their feelings with classmates.

For advanced students
- Discussion of a news item
- A film I can recommend
- Something I am proud of
- My plans for the week or the weekend

8.8 Today's special student

Aim   speaking, listening, building of a cohesive classroom environment

Level   intermediate–advanced

Time   10–15 minutes

Procedure

1 Every day or every other day, depending on the size of your class (you should get to all your students during the course of your session), choose a student who will be 'today's special student'.
2 The special student can choose the person who will introduce him/her.
3 The student and his/her introducer leave the room and prepare the introduction. (See Box 93 for an example.)

4 When they are ready they return and 'today's special student' is introduced and asked questions.

Box 93 Example of special student information

Today's special student is my friend Anna-Marie. Anna-Marie is from Switzerland and she loves to ski. She hopes to be able to study Medicine in the United States. As you all know, she is a very good student, and one reason she wants to study in America is that she loves the English language. Also her boyfriend, who is an engineer, is an American. Do you have any questions for Anna-Marie?

8.9 Celebrating birthdays

Aim speaking, writing, building of a cohesive classroom environment

Level all levels

Time 20–30 minutes

Procedure

1 On your class calendar (see activity 8.2) make a note of students' birthdays.
2 On a student's birthday, teach and sing 'the happy birthday song', and, in multilingual classes, ask students to sing their language birthday songs.
3 In small groups, students write a poem to the birthday student.
4 The poems are read out loud and are given to the birthday student. (For birthday poem pattern and example see Box 94.)

Box 94 Pattern for a birthday poem

Line one: first and last name of birthday student
Line two: three adjectives describing birthday student
Line three: three *ing* verbs that suit the birthday student
Line four: one sentence describing the birthday student
Line five: We are happy you are in our class.

Example poem:
Kumiko Nishimura
Small, lively, smart
Studying, running, succeeding
She is very ambitious
We are happy you are in our class!

Caveat: In Arab countries, birthdays have traditionally not been celebrated, but this does seem to be changing. However, I would check this out with students prior to making plans for a celebration.

8.10 The complaint/suggestion/compliment box

Aim	writing, class cohesion
Level	all levels
Time	fluid
Preparation	Prepare a large colorful box and place it in a visible place in the classroom.

Procedure

1 Encourage students to put suggestions and/or complaints/compliments about class or school life in the box. (This is a good activity for a group that finishes early.)
2 Periodically check the box, pulling out what you consider legitimate suggestions and have a class discussion on how they can best be implemented.

Note

I have seen this work successfully across ages and levels. An elementary teacher called it 'The Tattle Box'.

8.11 Elves and giants: an occasional on-going ritual

Aim   fluency practice, building of a cohesive classroom environment

Level   all levels

Time   four consecutive days

Procedure

1 Put the names of all students on slips of paper and place in a bag.
2 Each student draws a name.
3 The student who draws a name becomes the elf that serves the giant whose name is on the paper.
4 Each student thus becomes both an elf and a giant.
5 It is the job of the elves to do something nice for their giant during four consecutive days without letting the giant know who the elf is, for example, leaving a flower on the giant's desk.
6 On the fifth day the identities of all the elves are finally revealed and the class talks about how they felt during the week and how they feel about the activity. (See Box 95 for suggestions of nice things to be done for giants, and for ways of getting the things to the giants without disclosing the identity of the elf.)

Box 95 Suggestions for the elves and giants ritual

What one can do for the giants
- Buy them a candy bar
- Buy them a newspaper or a magazine
- Bring a flower
- Write a poem
- Draw a picture
- Bring a fruit
- Buy a pencil
- Buy a nice notebook
- Write a nice note
- Send a friendship card

How to get the gifts to the giants
- Ask the teacher to deliver
- Ask another student to deliver
- Put it under their chair
- Put it between their books
- Sneak it into their backpack

Bibliography

Aronson, Eliot (1996) *The Jigsaw Classroom*, Addison-Wesley.

Bassano, S. and Christison, M.A. (1995) *Community Spirit: A Practical Guide for Collaborative Language Learning*, ALTA.

Bassnet, S. and Grundy, P. (1993) *Language Through Literature: Creative Language Teaching through Literature*, Longman.

Brown, H.D. (1994) *Teaching by Principle: An Interactive Approach to Language Pedagogy*, Prentice Hall Regents.

Byrne, D. (1987) *Techniques for Classroom Interaction*, Longman.

Cisneros, Sandra (1985) *The House on Mango Street*, Artepublico Press.

Davis, P. and Rinvolucri, M. (1988) *Dictation: New methods, new possibilities*, Cambridge University Press.

Davis, P. and Rinvolucri, M. (1990) *The Confidence Book: Building Trust in the Language Classroom*, Longman.

Davis, P. and Rinvolucri, M. (1995) *More Grammar Games: Cognitive, Affective, and Drama Activities of EFL students*, Cambridge University Press.

Davis Samway, K., Whang, G. and Pippitt, M. (1995) *Buddy Reading: Cross-Age Tutoring in a Multicultural School*, Heinemann.

Frank, C. and Rinvolucri, M. (1983) *Grammar in Action: Awareness Activities for Language Learning*, Pergamon Press.

Frost, R. (1916) 'The Road not Taken' in *The Poetry of Robert Frost*, New York: Holt Rinehart and Winston, 1967.

Grant, N. (1987) *Making the Most of Your Textbook*, Longman.

Greenwood, J. (1988) *Class Readers*, Oxford University Press.

Hess, N. (1991) *Headstarts: One Hundred Original Pre-Text Activities*, Longman.

Hess, N. and Pollard, L. (1995) *Creative Questions: Lively Uses of the Interrogative*, Longman.

Hill, D. (1990) *Visual Impact: Creative Language Learning through Pictures*, Longman.

Joyce, J. (1914) 'Eveline' in *The Dubliners*, London: Grant Richards.

Klippel, F. (1984) *Keep Talking: Communicative Fluency Activities for Language Learning*, Cambridge University Press.

Lazar, G. (1993) *Literature and Language Teaching: A Guide for Teachers and Trainers*, Cambridge University Press.

Lewis, M. (1993) *The Lexical Approach: The State of ELT and a Way Forward*, Language Teaching Publications.

Morgan, J. and Rinvolucri, M. (1986) *Vocabulary*, Oxford University Press.

Peregoy, S.F. and Boyle, O. (1997) *Reading, Writing, & Learning in ESL: A Resource Book for Teachers*, Longman.

Pollard, L. and Hess, N. (1997) *Zero Prep: Ready-to-Go Activities for the Language Classroom*, ALTA.

Rinvolucri, M. (1984) *Grammar Games: Cognitive, Affective, and Drama Activities of EFL students*, Cambridge University Press.

Silberstein, S. (1994) *Techniques and Resources in Teaching Reading*, Oxford University Press.

Ur, P. (1988) *Grammar Practice Activities: A Practical Guide for Teachers*, Cambridge University Press.

Ur, P. (1981) *Discussions That Work: Task-centered fluency practice*, Cambridge University Press.

Ur, P. (1984) *Teaching Listening Comprehension*, Cambridge University Press.

Whitson, V. (1996) *New Ways of Using Drama and Literature in Language Learning*, TESOL.

Woodward, T. and Lindstromberg, S. (1995) *Planning from Lesson to Lesson: A Way of Making Lesson Planning Easier*, Longman.

Index

absent student notebook 188
attendance, taking 5, 22–3, 183, 186–7

benefits and challenges 2–6

categorizing 75–6
challenges 4–6
class calendar 185–6
class cohesion 18, 26–7, 38–43, 44–50,
    55–7, 59, 65–6, 68–9, 145–52,
    153–6, 157–8, 188–93
class goals 68–9, 183–5
class rituals 183, 189–93
class to class communication 83–4
classroom management 4, 5, 14, 22–3,
    79–80, 113–18, 178–9, 182–9
collaboration 10–12, 105–6, 118–19
    see also group work; writing: collaborative
commonly used expressions 172–3
community projects 11, 94–5, 127–9
confidence 34, 145–6
control 4–5, 15, 113–14
coping principles 7–15
course packs 183

dialogue practice 113
discussions 60–1, 83–4, 85, 113, 118–19,
    124–5

enlarging the circle 14–15

family relations 10, 20, 33, 155
film previews 131
fluency practice 17–18, 23, 26–32, 38–41,
    44–50, 55–7, 58–9, 64–5, 66–7, 68–73,
    83–4, 93, 102–3, 105–9, 110–11,
    115–26, 127–9, 130–1, 135, 139,
    143–4, 145–50, 151–6, 157–8, 160–6,
    169, 172–4, 178, 183–6, 189–90, 193
friendships 10, 44–6

getting to know students 20, 24–33, 86–7,
    91–2, 95–6, 146–7, 155–6, 190–2
    see also names, learning students'
'good folders' 156–7
grade contracts 178–9
grammar review 110–11, 113, 133–4, 136
group work 11, 112–15
    cohesion 135
    content based activities 119–36
    cooperation 115–16, 125–6
    organizational activities 115–19
    participation 114, 118–19
    roles 114, 115–16
    see also writing: collaborative

home 10, 98
homework check 129–30, 186–7

individual expression 150–6
individualization 6, 12, 137, 138–44
interest 9–10, 15, 35, 137
introducing new topics 69–70

jigsaw activities 11, 119–22

learning
    clarifying commitments 162–3, 164–5
    goals 68–9, 161–2, 165–6, 169, 183–5
    languages 62–3, 160, 177
    personal conferences 25, 165–6
    risk-taking 171–2
    student responsibility for 159–81, 182,
        186–7
    styles 6, 159–61, 169–70, 176–7
    teacher's role 162–4, 165–6
lesson plans 15, 187
lesson starters 189–90
listening 29–32, 41–4, 73–5, 81–2, 121–3,
    190–1
    to dictations 73–4, 126–7, 138–9
    to directions 116–18
    improving skills 56, 129–30, 143–4,
        166–8, 176–7
    interviews 28–9

motivation 34, 137

names, learning students' 16–23
    see also getting to know students
native language use 114
newspapers, using 29–31, 57–8

open-endedness 13–14
organizing material 51–4

pace 9
pair work 11, 109–10, 113, 117
peer teaching 3, 183
    see also writing: peer reviews
personal conferences 25, 165–6
personalization 12–13, 137, 144–58
personalized dictionaries 12
portfolio projects 12
poster presentations 11, 12, 13, 18,
    29–31, 64–5, 146–7
problem solving 59, 113
proficiency levels 1–2

question formation 26–7, 60–1, 63–4, 85,
    136, 175–6
question strategies 14
quiet signals 116–18
quiet students, activating 6, 14–15, 34–5,
    114, 118–19

reading 24, 78–9

aloud 73–4, 75, 80–2, 129–30, 131–2, 136, 175–6
extensive 127–9
individualized 139, 156–7, 169–70, 180–1
interpreting 60–1, 80–1, 91–2, 157–8
jigsaws 119–21
predicting 136
questioning 143–4
reviews 139–40, 152
scanning for information 57–8, 133–4, 183–6, 187
summaries 67
talking about 26–7, 41–4, 50–1
research 98, 127–9
reviewing 43–4, 54, 62–76, 126–7, 129–30, 131–2, 187
see also grammar review
routines see class rituals; classroom management

self-access centers 12, 140–2
self-correction 173–4
sentence practice 22, 58–9, 92–3, 99, 122–3, 143
sharing ideas 40–1, 87–8, 89–90, 91–3
sharing information 43–4, 87–8, 143–4
sharing opinions 80–1
silences 15
size of class 1–2
speaking 34–5
  circle talk 55–6
  clarity 59–60, 73–4, 126–7
  explaining 20, 31–2, 43–4, 51–4, 74, 119–20, 134, 176–7
  expressing opinions 34–43, 50–1
  interviews 28–9
  introductions 32–3, 113, 190–1
  questions and answers 30–1, 129–30
  self-correction 173–4
  three minute speeches 145–6
  and writing 78–9, 85
  see also fluency practice
summarizing skills 64–5, 67, 119–20
syllabus 183–5

tardiness 186–7
time management (topic) 10, 31–2

variety 3, 4, 8–9, 113
Venn diagrams 71–2
vocabulary
  adjectives 21, 50, 72–3, 95–6
  drill 113
  expansion 22, 58–9, 68, 122–3, 133, 134, 135, 175
  individual practice 142–3

nouns 75–6
personalization 144–5
reinforcement 17, 121–2
review 69–70, 132, 136, 149–50, 153, 157
verbs 95–6

who (relative pronoun) 154–5
writing
  buddy journals 11, 86–7
  chat rooms 89–90
  for clarity 186–7
  clustering 102–3
  collaborative 11, 54, 66–7, 80–1, 92–3, 130, 134
  complaints/suggestions/compliments 192
  completion 39–40
  conferences 25, 83–4
  cultivating pride in 88–9
  dictations 59–60, 73–4, 126–7, 136, 138–9
  email 87–8
  exit notes 188–9
  feedback 5–6, 79
  flip-flop books 51–2
  folders 97
  genres 100–1
  importance of 77
  individualization 12, 23, 91–2, 160–5, 169, 178
  jigsaw activities 119–22
  letter formation 19, 77
  letters 13, 24–5, 105–6, 107, 150–1
  outlines 43–4
  peer reviews 5–6, 11, 79, 80, 81–2
  personalized guide books 98, 100
  poems 95–6, 191–2
  practical tips 79–80
  practice 78
  process 103–4
  prompts for discussion 85
  questions 63–4
  quizzes 65–6
  reports 139–40
  self-correction 80, 97, 104–5, 173–4, 180–1
  service writing 94–5
  spelling 109–10, 138–9, 173–4
  stories 93, 98, 99, 106, 108–9, 110–11, 121–2, 123
  supporting excellence 88–9
  as talking 78
  teaching 77–80
  using web-sites 12, 90–1
  wall newspapers 88–9
  see also poster presentations